MiG
Red Star Fighters

Since its foundation in the late 1930s more than 55,000 aircraft – of over 400 sub-types – have been produced by the MiG Design Bureau. From Artem Mikoyan's 25hp Oktyabrenok of 1937 to the Mach 2.8-capable MiG-31 *Foxhound* and the next generation of 21st Century MiG-35s, this publication is a tribute to the designers, engineers and crews who have flown and operated the most-famous of Soviet military aircraft.

Stephen Bridgewater
Stamford, January 2018

As well as serving extensively with the Soviet Air Force MiG fighters have been exported widely to 'friendly' nations. These Romanian MiG-15s are preparing for a training sortie at the height of the Cold War.

CONTENTS

4 Mikoyan & Gurevich – Legendary Designers
Steve Bridgewater looks back at the pre-war history that led to the creation of the MiG Design Bureau

8 MiG Pistons
Although best known as a manufacturer of Cold War jets, MiG OKB produced thousands of piston-powered fighters and several intriguing prototypes during World War Two

18 MiG Enters the Jet Age
With Britain, Germany and the USA all having jet fighters by the end of World War Two, it was inevitable that the USSR would follow suit. Steve Bridgewater investigates the history of the MiG-9 *Fargo*

24 Swept Wing MiGs
The incomparable MiG-15 was the Design Bureau's breakthrough jet fighter. While internationally influenced, it's nothing less than a Soviet icon. Paul Fiddian looks at the making of a legend and the MiG-17 it spawned

32 The Victorious Underdog
On August 9, 1952, at the height of the Korean War, Cmdr Peter 'Hoagy' Carmichael achieved notoriety by shooting down a MiG-15 jet with a piston-powered Sea Fury. Kimberley Hawkins looks at the controversial kill

34 The Fighting *Farmer*
Overshadowed by its more famous brethren, the MiG-19 was widely exported and flown by 27 nations around the world. Todd Shugart explains why the Russian *Farmer* deserves greater recognition

40 Moolah For MiGs
At the height of the Korean War the USA desperately wanted to get its hands on a serviceable example of the new MiG-15. Steven Taylor looks at a three-year campaign of subterfuge, espionage and good old-fashioned bribery

46 Project *Have Doughnut*
De-classified documents reveal the extent to which the USAF clandestinely tested a MiG-21 at Groom Lake, Nevada

52 MiG's Fabulous *Fishbed*
The most-produced supersonic jet aircraft in aviation history and the most-manufactured combat aircraft since the Korean War, the MiG-21 served with more than 60 air arms on four continents and remains in service with more than a dozen nations

62 Swing-Wing MiGs
Paul Fiddian discusses the development and operational history of the fighter-bomber and ground attack variants of the MiG-23 and MiG-27 *Flogger*

68 MiG's Fantastic *Fulcrum*
The MiG-29 is one of the most capable fighters the world has ever seen. Paul Fiddian and Steve Bridgewater turn their attention towards the past, present and future of the *Fulcrum*

76 *Foxbat* out of Hell
In 1976 an audacious Russian pilot defected to Japan in a Soviet MiG-25 Foxbat. Steven Taylor tells the story of this incredible event, which caused consternation in Moscow and a sensation in the West

82 "A Wanton Attack"
That was how a furious Winston Churchill described the shooting down of an RAF Avro Lincoln by Soviet MiG-15s in March 1953. But almost 70 years on, mystery still surrounds the RAF's first Cold War loss. Steven Taylor investigates

88 *Foxhound* – Russia's Game Changer
Dr Dave Sloggett explores the transformative effect the MiG-31 supersonic interceptor has had on the Russian Air Force

94 21st Century MiG
Despite its prominence in the 1970s and 80s the MiG Design Bureau has failed to win any major aircraft tenders in the post-Soviet era, but this is not for the want of creating some truly memorable and promising designs, as Steve Bridgewater reveals

98 Museum MiGs
Jamie Ewan presents a roundup of MiGs on display in British museums

---

Editor: Stephen Bridgewater
2023 Updates: Paul Hamblin
Senior editor, specials: Roger Mortimer
Email: roger.mortimer@keypublishing.com
Cover design: Steve Donovan
Design: Paul Silk
Advertising Sales Manager: Brodie Baxter
Email: brodie.baxter@keypublishing.com
Tel: 01780 755131
Advertising Production: Debi McGowan
Email: debi.mcgowan@keypublishing.com

SUBSCRIPTION/MAIL ORDER
Key Publishing Ltd, PO Box 300, Stamford, Lincs, PE9 1NA
Tel: 01780 480404
Subscriptions email: subs@keypublishing.com

Mail Order email:
orders@keypublishing.com
Website: www.keypublishing.com/shop

PUBLISHING
Group CEO: Adrian Cox
Publisher, Books and Bookazines: Jonathan Jackson
Published by
Key Publishing Ltd, PO Box 100, Stamford, Lincs, PE9 1XQ
Tel: 01780 755131
Website: www.keypublishing.com

PRINTING
Precision Colour Printing Ltd, Haldane, Halesfield 1, Telford, Shropshire. TF7 4QQ

DISTRIBUTION
Seymour Distribution Ltd, 2 Poultry Avenue, London, EC1A 9PU
Enquiries Line: 02074 294000.

ISBN: 978 1 80282 757 6
All images via the Key Publishing Archive unless stated

We are unable to guarantee the bonafides of any of our advertisers. Readers are strongly recommended to take their own precautions before parting with any information or item of value, including, but not limited to money, manuscripts, photographs, or personal information in response to any advertisements within this publication.

© Key Publishing Ltd 2023
All rights reserved. No part of this magazine may be reproduced or transmitted in any form by any means, electronic or mechanical, including photocopying, recording or by any information storage and retrieval system, without prior permission in writing from the copyright owner. Multiple copying of the contents of the magazine without prior written approval is not permitted.

The Early Years
Mikoyan & Gurevich – Legendary Designers

Since its foundation in the late 1930s, the MiG Design Bureau has produced more than 55,000 aircraft of more than 400 sub-types. Steve Bridgewater looks back at the pre-war history that led to the creation of this legendary aircraft manufacturer.

Based upon the initial drawings completed in collaboration with Nikolai Polikarpov, the I-200 evolved into a very attractive and purposeful fighter. It was a low-wing monoplane with a hydraulically retractable tailwheel undercarriage. Due to shortages of light alloys the aircraft was of mixed construction. The rear fuselage was made from wood, but the front fuselage, from the propeller to the rear of the cockpit, was a welded steel tube truss covered by duralumin. The cockpit itself was situated well aft, in a style typical of aircraft designed by the Polikarpov design bureau.

Although the term 'MiG' is synonymous with the Cold War the company that produced these iconic fighters traces its history back to December 1939 when it was created as an independent design department by Artem Ivanovich Mikoyan, a young aviation designer who had grown up in a remote village near Sanahin in present-day Armenia.

Mikoyan was born on August 5, 1905 and after leaving school he took a job as a machine-tool operator in Rostov before briefly working in Moscow's Dynamo factory. Then, in 1931, he was briefly conscripted into the military before joining the Zhukovsky Air Force Academy. He soon demonstrated a keen understanding of aerodynamics and aircraft design and in 1935 he was allocated to the Kharkov establishment as a 'work experience' apprentice.

It was during this time that Mikoyan joined forces with fellow student K Samarin to produce his first independently designed aircraft. Christened the Oktyabrenok, the single-engined sports aircraft had a parasol wing and a well-worn 25hp Labur engine that had been donated by a lecturer. It would be November 1937 before the

Artem Ivanovich Mikoyan (August 5, 1905 – December 9, 1970) and Mikhail Iosifovich Gurevich (January 12, 1893 – November 12, 1976). Founders of the Mikoyan-Gurevich design bureau.

Oktyabrenok took flight and although test pilot VV Bubnov reported favourably on the handling characteristics, the engine quit on the fourth flight and the aircraft was damaged.

By now Mikoyan's skills had been recognised by Soviet aircraft designer Nikolai Polikarpov and upon graduation from Zhukovsky he joined the Polikarpov Design Bureau at Vnukovo, Moscow. As such all thoughts of the Oktyabrenok were abandoned.

At Polikarpov, Mikoyan was initially employed as an inspector of recently completed aircraft and he often fed back suggestions and observations about the quality of the machines he received. This insight was not lost on the chief designer, who quickly requested that Mikoyan be given more specific duties. Polikarpov therefore gave the 32-year-old fledgling designer the opportunity to prove his worth – by independently assessing the powerplant and machine gun systems fitted on the first I 153 fighters. The new aircraft were hampered by overheating engines and jamming weapons and while the munitions issue remained unsolved, Mikoyan cured the engine problem within weeks.

MIKOYAN MEETS GUREVICH
It was during his work on the I-153 that Mikoyan was introduced to and befriended by Polikarpov's deputy bureau chief – Mikhail Iosifovich Gurevich.

Gurevich had been born on January 12, 1893 in Rubanshchina, a village in Ukraine's Kursk region. From a financially secure family (the son of a winery mechanic) the young Gurevich had pursued a career in aerospace by studying mathematics at the Kharkiv University from

Left: In 1935, Mikoyan was allocated to the Kharkov establishment as a 'work experience' apprentice. It was during this time that he joined forces with fellow student K Samarin to produce his first independently designed aircraft (pictured in the foreground).
Right: At Polikarpov, Mikoyan primarily worked on the I-153 fighter programme, which was hampered by overheating engines and jamming weapons. While the munitions issue remained unsolved, Mikoyan cured the engine problem within weeks.

1910. However, after just a year he was expelled for taking part in "revolutionary activities against the ruling monarchy" and moved to France to continue his studies at the University of Montpellier.

Gurevich returned to Russia in 1914 and eventually graduated from the Kharkiv Technological Institute in 1923 before joining the Polikarpov Design Bureau.

Over the coming years he was involved in a number of projects, including the stillborn TOM-1 Open Sea Torpedo Carrier and the TSh-3 ground attack aircraft. Perhaps his most noteworthy achievement during this period was his 1936 journey to the USA to negotiate a licence to produce the Douglas DC-3 passenger aircraft in Russia but by the time he met Artem Mikoyan in 1938 Gurevich was effectively Polikarpov's second in command at Vnukovo.

In March 1939 Mikoyan was appointed as chief design engineer on the I-153 programme and found himself working with his friend on an even closer basis. The two formed a powerful team, with the younger Mikoyan demonstrating both radical thinking and excellent leadership skills and the older, more experienced Gurevich offering a sober-minded approach with years of hands-on experience that enabled him to know what could realistically be achieved.

NEW GENERATION

By the late 1930s all was not well at the Polikarpov Design Bureau. Elsewhere in the world, the fighter aircraft had evolved from 'rag and tube' biplanes to all-metal monoplanes but Polikarpov had failed to keep up with development. Although the I-153 boasted a modern retractable undercarriage it was a draggy biplane with a maximum speed of just 243kts (280mph). The later Polikarpov I-16 'Rata' monoplane could reach 283kts (326mph) but lacked the manoeuvrability of its biplane ancestor.

"The two formed a powerful team"

In 1938 Nikolai Polikarpov announced the creation of the I-180 – a last ditch attempt to extract vital performance from the I-16 airframe. The aircraft was still a single-engined, low-wing monoplane aircraft and had mixed construction with a duralumin frame covered in plywood and fabric. The landing gear was still retracted pneumatically but now the tailwheel retracted too. The main visual difference between the I-180 and I-16 was a new wing with a perpendicular straight leading edge, an aerodynamically refined fuselage featuring an enclosed cockpit and a longer, slimmer engine cowling housing a 1,100hp M-88 engine; itself a developed and licence-built Gnome-Rhône Mistral Major. Armament consisted of four 0.3in (7.62mm) ShKAS machine guns and 440lbs (200kg) of bombs.

The aircraft was beset with problems and delays from the outset. The propeller was delayed, and early test runs were conducted using a different propeller with manual pitch control. Consequently, the engine was prone to overheating, and to compensate for this the cowling flaps restricting airflow around the engine were removed.

Despite these problems, and the fact that the prototype had not completed its ground tests, the authorities were demanding a test flight as soon as possible. Polikarpov himself objected to flying the prototype before it would be ready - which he estimated to be in February 1939. However, on December 15, 1938 the famous Soviet test pilot Valery Chkalov took the I-180 into the sky for the first time. Neither Polikarpov nor lead designer Dmitriy Tomashevich approved the flight, and neither had signed the form releasing the prototype from the factory.

Despite the flight plan forbidding the pilot climbing above 1,970ft (600m) Chkalov took the new fighter up to 6,560ft (2,000m) before returning to land. It is thought he miscalculated his landing approach and came in short of the airfield but, when he attempted to correct the flight path, the engine quit and the I-180 crashed into a powerline. Chkalov was thrown from the cockpit, badly injured, and died two hours later.

The official government investigation concluded that the engine quit because it became too cold in the absence of the cowl flaps. As the result of the crash, Tomashevich and several other officials, including Arms Industry Department Director S Belyakin, who urged the first flight, were immediately arrested. Although

By the late 1930s, most fighter aircraft had evolved from 'rag and tube' biplanes to all-metal monoplanes but Polikarpov had failed to keep up with development. Although the I-153 boasted a modern retractable undercarriage it was a draggy biplane. The later Polikarpov I-16 'Rata' monoplane (illustrated) could reach 283kts but lacked the manoeuvrability of its biplane ancestor.

In 1938, Polikarpov announced the creation of the I-180 – a last ditch attempt to extract vital performance from the I-16 airframe. The main visual differences were a new wing with a perpendicular straight leading edge, an aerodynamically refined fuselage with an enclosed cockpit and a longer, slimmer engine cowling housing a 1,100hp M-88 engine.

It would be November 1937 before the Oktyabrenok took flight and although test pilot V V Bubnov reported favourably on the handling characteristics, the engine quit on the fourth flight and the aircraft was damaged. By now, Mikoyan's skills had been recognised by Soviet aircraft designer Nikolai Polikarpov and all thoughts of the Oktyabrenok were abandoned.

Nikolai Polikarpov escaped arrest his reputation with Joseph Stalin suffered a blow from which he would never recover.

The second prototype flew on April 27, 1939 but crashed on September 5 killing the pilot and then, on May 26, 1940 the second production I-180S also fell from the sky. By the time the third prototype I-180 also crashed on July 6, 1940 Polikarpov had lost faith in his own abilities and the chain of accidents soon aroused suspicion of sabotage resulting in further arrests.

It was the beginning of the end for the once dominant company and towards the end of the year Polikarpov was told the I-180 project was to be terminated and that his factory would produce Lavochkin LaGG-3 fighters instead.

PROJECT K

In the meantime, Russian test pilots had been evaluating fighter aircraft sourced from abroad. Between 1937 and 1939, crews had flown aircraft as diverse as the German Messerschmitt Bf 109, the American Seversky P-35, the Japanese Mitsubishi Type 96 and the French Dewoitine 510. As a result, a number of esteemed Soviet test pilots wrote to the Central Committee for Aviation criticising the state of their nation's fighter aircraft.

An emergency meeting was called at the Kremlin in February 1939 with aircraft and engine designers summoned to explain what they were doing to remedy the situation. In attendance were the likes of Sergei Ilyushin, Aleksandr Arkhangelsky, Aleksandr Klimov, Aleksandr Mikulin, Arkadi Shvetsov, Aleksandr Yakovlev, Pavel Sukhoi and Nikolai Polikarpov himself – all of whom were asked to submit proposals for new combat aircraft.

Although Messrs Mikoyan and Gurevich were yet to form their own design bureau (and were therefore not invited to the high-level conference) they had plenty of input to feed via their boss at Polikarpov.

The two had cleverly distanced themselves from the ill-fated I-180 programme and had been working on what was dubbed 'Project K.' This was a high-altitude interceptor aircraft to be powered by the new Mikulin AM-37 engine and the duo claimed the aircraft could boast a maximum speed as high as 360kts (416mph). The aircraft had come about after Aleksandr Mikulin had approached Polikarpov to offer the use of his latest engine, which had been rejected by other design bureaus because they believed it was too heavy. However, Polikarpov, Mikoyan and Gurevich saw the powerplant's potential to operate at high altitude and incorporated it into a proposed fighter to appease the Central Committee's next Kremlin meeting.

BREAKAWAY GROUP

By late 1939 production of the Polikarpov I-153 and I-16 had halted at Vnukovo and with the I-180 programme eventually cancelled too the factory was employed to produce limited numbers of Yakovlev BB-22 bombers.

> "Polikarpov lost faith in his abilities and the chain of accidents aroused suspicion of sabotage"

However, in late November a committee of government officials visited to decide the future of the plant. Nikolai Polikarpov was working in Germany at the time and Artem Mikoyan was recovering from serious illness but Mikhail Gurevich's impassioned presentation convinced the committee of the viability of the 'Project K' programme.

On December 8, 1939, a special bureau detachment was created under the leadership of Artem Mikoyan – whose brother Anastas was now a senior politician in Joseph Stalin's Communist Party.

Mikoyan would be supported in his new design bureau by Gurevich and Vladimir Romodin, both of whom would work as his deputies. All existing Polikarpov employees were given the choice of staying in their existing jobs or transferring to the new Mikoyan company. Some 40% chose to make the move and when Nikolai Polikarpov returned from Germany he was distraught to discover his work force decimated and large portions of his factory had been taken over by the newly formed bureau.

Polikarpov was subsequently appointed as a professor at the Moscow Aviation Institute but would never truly recover from the events of 1939. He died on July 30, 1944 from stomach cancer.

Back at Vnukovo the newly formed Mikoyan Design Bureau (OKB) was quickly assigned two urgent projects – the production of a high-altitude fighter (based on the 'Project K' research) and the development of a two-seat ground attack aircraft, both of which were to be powered by variants of the Mikulin powerplant.

Priority was given to the fighter and the Central Committee called for a prototype to fly by mid-April 1940 – just over four months from the creation of the company itself.

The fighter – by now dubbed the I-200 – was developed under the threat of imminent war and with rapid and pleasing progress noted by the government the decision was made to formulate the Mikoyan bureau detachment (which was still effectively a branch of the Polikarpov company) into a fully recognised experimental design bureau. It was at this point that Artem Mikoyan insisted that his friend and colleague's name also appear in the organisation's title – and the Mikoyan-Gurevich (or MiG) Experimental Design Bureau was officially born.

THE FIRST MiG

The I-200 was designed to tight specifications and was to be capable of both fighter/interceptor roles as well as long-range escort work. The first components were produced in late December 1939 and the prototype was beginning to take shape by the end of January.

Based upon the initial drawings completed in collaboration with Nikolai Polikarpov, the I-200 evolved into a very attractive and purposeful fighter. It was a low-wing monoplane with a hydraulically retractable tailwheel undercarriage. Due to shortages of light alloys the aircraft was of mixed construction. The rear fuselage was made from wood, but the front fuselage, from the propeller to the rear of the cockpit, was a welded steel tube truss covered by duralumin. The cockpit itself was situated well aft, in a style typical of aircraft designed by the Polikarpov Design Bureau.

The bulk of the wing was wooden, but the centre-section was all-metal with a steel I-section main spar. The wing used a Clark Y profile and was evenly tapered with rounded tips. The outer wing panels featured five degrees of dihedral.

Crucially, Mikulin's much anticipated AM-37 engine was not yet available so the prototype was designed around the less powerful 1,350hp AM-35A V-12 powerplant. The engine was supercharged (with air coming from intakes in the wing roots) and drove a 9ft 8in (2.98m) diameter variable pitch VISh-22Ye propeller. The radiator was underneath the cockpit.

The prototype I-200 was shipped to Khodynka Aerodrome in Moscow on March 31, 1940 for testing. On April 5, test pilot Arkadiy Yekatov took the aircraft into the skies for the first time – ten days ahead of the government enforced deadline. Establishing a new Soviet speed record of 350kts on May 24, the airframe would later become known as the MiG-1.

Armament included two fuselage-mounted .30in (7.62mm) ShKAS machine guns and one .50in (12.7mm) UBS machine gun.

The entire MiG Bureau worked efficiently and despite the incredibly tight schedule, the prototype was shipped to Khodynka Aerodrome in Moscow on March 31, 1940 for testing. On April 5, test pilot Arkadiy Yekatov took the aircraft into the skies for the first time – ten days ahead of the government enforced deadline. On May 1, it appeared in public for the first time at the Red Square May Day Parade and with its performance continuing to impress it established a new Soviet speed record of 350kts (403mph) on May 24 – a figure that staggered the Soviet Air Force (Voyenno-Vozdushnye Sily or VVS), whose fastest fighters of the day struggled to exceed 321kts (370mph).

In the meantime, a second example had performed its maiden flight on May 9 (with A P Yakushev at the controls) and a third prototype (the first to be armed) made its first flight on June 6 with Aleksandr Zhukov at the helm.

DEFICIENCIES

The I-200 was undoubtedly fast and could also climb quickly – in fact it could reach 16,000ft (4,877m) in just 5 minutes – but testing by VVS test pilots between August 29 and September 12, 1940 revealed a number of deficiencies.

In simulated dogfights the aircraft demonstrated poor stability (including a dangerous propensity to flick from a simple stall into a spin from which it was almost impossible to recover) and inadequate visibility from the tightly enclosed canopy. On the ground, the canopy proved difficult to open and close and the brakes were also highlighted as unreliable.

Most critically, crews reported problems with cockpit ventilation. To make matters worse the aircraft's radiator was mounted just below the pilot's seat with boiling coolant making the cockpit even hotter. Even though the water and oil cooling systems were redesigned 14 and 17 times respectively, cockpit temperatures remained unacceptable and test pilots also voiced concerns about the possibility of being scalded by a leaking radiator.

Nonetheless, the aircraft remained a consistently good performer and its handling and cooling issues were largely ignored in an attempt to rush it into front-line service. In the autumn, the aircraft was approved for serial manufacture, with the proviso that production versions had a number of modifications. These included: greater longitudinal and transverse stability, reduced stick forces, rubber sheaths around the fuel tanks to make them self-sealing, better wheels (including a rubberised tailwheel), wing slats, two underwing bomb racks each capable of carrying a 220lb (100kg) FAB-100 bomb, two more (removable) guns and an increased fuel capacity to enable a minimum range of 621 miles (1,000km).

> **"The cumbersome canopy could only be opened by ground crews as it latched from the outside"**

Other aircraft competing for fighter contracts at the time included the Yakovlev I-26 (which became the Yak-1) and the Lavochkin I-301 (LaGG-3). Polikarpov's aforementioned I-180 had by now fallen completely out of favour although designer Nikolai Polikarpov's input into the I-200 design was ultimately recognised with a state award.

The first example of the AM-37 engine was finally available from late 1940 and was retrofitted into the second prototype I-200. The aircraft first flew with the powerplant on January 6, 1941 but experienced severe vibration problems and, despite efforts to cure the problems, the engine failed during a flight on May 7. Both aircraft and engine were destroyed.

The third prototype was mostly used for armament trials and was fitted at various times with 3.2in (82mm) RS-82 rockets and the experimental 0.91in (23mm) MP-3 and MP-6 autocannons, both of which were carried underneath the wings. Testing of the latter revealed very unsatisfactory performance from the guns and their development was cancelled. The designers were arrested and executed!

INTO SERVICE

The first I-200s entered service with the VVS on December 3, 1940 when the 41st Fighter Regiment, based in the Crimean town of Kacha, was ordered to conduct operational trials with the type.

Not unexpectedly, pilots had many complaints about the type; most notably regarding the cockpit temperatures and the cumbersome canopy – which opened to the side and could therefore only be operated on the ground. Worse still, it could only be opened by ground crews as it latched from the outside. Many pilots therefore elected to remove the canopy completely, allowing them to vacate the aircraft in a hurry if needed – but at the expense of between 11 and 14kts (12 and 16mph) of speed.

Eventually, MiG began delivering new versions of the fighter with a rear sliding canopy that could be jettisoned in flight but the company was unable to remedy the pilots' other main gripe – the aircraft's woefully inadequate stability.

In certain parts of the flight envelope – particularly with a high angle of attack – the aircraft was very difficult to control and pilots needed to give the I-200 their constant attention in order to avoid it flicking into an unrecoverable spin.

On January 6, 1941, a written order from the VVS decreed that the I-200 would from now on be referred to as the MiG-1, in tribute to the company's two remaining lead designers and in keeping with a new air force wide programme of renaming aircraft. The designation took the first letters of each of their surnames and joined them with an 'I' (the Russian word for 'and').

By the end of February 1941, a total of 89 MiG-1s had been delivered. Many of these went to the 146th Fighter Regiment at Yevpatoria, Crimea for pilot training with others joining regular fighter units such as the 89th Fighter Regiment at Kaunas, Lithuania and the 41st Fighter Regiment at Białystok, Poland. By June, just 55 remained operational, including eight assigned to the Soviet Navy.

The MiG-1 continued to evolve and the improvement process continued throughout the aircraft's lifespan. However, the changes were not immediately implemented in the production line, but were instead incorporated in a fourth prototype, which first flew on October 29, 1940 and was a significant improvement over the I-200s then in production. It passed its State acceptance trials and its improvements were incorporated in the production line from the 101st example. These were designated as the MiG-3 on December 9, although the first production MiG-3 was not completed until December 20.

Little is known of the performance of the MiG-1 in combat but most are thought likely to have been destroyed during the opening days of Operation *Barbarossa*, the German invasion of the Soviet Union in June 1941.

MiG PISTONS

Although best known as a manufacturer of Cold War jets, the MiG OKB produced thousands of piston-powered fighters and several intriguing prototypes during World War Two, as Steve Bridgewater reveals.

In recent years a small number of MiG-3s have been restored for private collectors. Rebuilt from wreckage of original Mikoyan-built machines these modern representations are fitted with US-design Allison engines in place of the rare and unreliable Mikulin powerplant. *Neil Harris*

Despite its shortcomings the initial MiG-1s proved capable and popular with pilots who knew how to fly them well. Therefore, hopes were high for the updated and improved version.

In order to address the stability deficiencies in the earlier design, a full-size model was built and tested in the T-1 wind tunnel belonging to the Central Aero and Hydrodynamics Institute in Moscow. The defects noted during testing forced Mikoyan and Gurevich to make a number of modifications to the design.

Lateral stability was improved by increasing the dihedral on the outer wing panels by a further one degree and the engine was moved forwards by 4in (10cm) to improve longitudinal stability. This increased the length of the fuselage and the designers found that if a new water radiator was also fitted, enough room was created to allow an additional 66 US Gal (250lit) fuel tank to be fitted beneath the pilot's seat and an extra oil tank to be mounted below the engine.

Piping was fitted to feed cooled inert exhaust gasses into the fuel tanks to reduce the chance of fire and another safety measure saw the back of the pilot's seat armoured with a 0.31in (8mm) steel plate.

Other changes included streamlining the supercharger intakes, strengthening the main landing gear, increasing the size of the main wheels and extending the canopy glazing aft to improve the view to the rear. The latter also allowed for the installation of a shelf behind the pilot for an RSI-1 radio.

An improved gunsight and upgraded instrument panel were also fitted and the ammunition increased to 750 rounds per gun. Finally, two additional underwing hardpoints were added to carry up to 485lbs (220kg) of bombs, spray containers or RS-82 rockets.

Despite its shortcomings the initial MiG-1s proved capable and popular with pilots who knew how to fly them well. Therefore, hopes were high for the updated and improved version.

MiG-3

The modified aircraft first flew on October 29, 1940 and was initially classified as the fourth prototype I-200/MiG-1, but it was so significantly different to the earlier design that it was dubbed the MiG-3 after passing State acceptance trials in December. Although it was only the second aircraft designed by the new design bureau, the naming decision was based on the fact that the Communist rulers had decreed that fighter aircraft should have odd number designations and bombers would be given even numbers.

Twenty examples of the new MiG-3 were delivered before the end of the year and Vnukovo's Zavod (Factory) No 1 would produce large numbers in 1941 before it was re-tasked with producing Il-2 Shturmoviks for rival company Ilyushin.

Acceptance trials took place between January 27 and February 26, 1941 and the MiG-3 was found to be more than 550lbs (250kg) heavier than the earlier MiG-1. This in turn resulted in both reduced manoeuvrability and general performance. The time it took to climb to 16,000ft (4,879m) increased by more than a minute and the service ceiling was reduced by more than 1,500ft (457m). However, on the up-side the MiG-3 was faster than

> "Soviet rulers awarded Mikhail Gurevich the State Stalin Prize"

its predecessor both at sea level and at altitude. Range was greater than the MiG-1 but still less than the required 621 miles (1,000km). Despite these deficiencies the Soviet rulers awarded Mikhail Gurevich the State Stalin Prize for his contribution to aviation.

QUALITY CONTROL EXECUTION

As aircraft reached the VVS regiments a number of reports began to be received about the poor quality of some of the airframes. These were referred to the NII VVS (air force research institute), which was responsible for monitoring the quality of the aircraft delivered to the VVS. On May 31, 1941, the People's Commissariat of Defence decreed that the NII VVS had been negligent. A number of senior managers were demoted and the head of the Institute, Major General A I Filin was summarily executed!

Among the problems found with early MiG-3s were unacceptable levels of performance at high altitude. Despite being designed primarily as a high-altitude interceptor, the oxygen supply was often insufficient and the stall and spin characteristics in the thinner upper air were very dangerous, especially to inexperienced pilots. This was demonstrated on April 10, 1941, when three pilots of the 31st Fighter Regiment of the Air Defences (IAP PVO) attempted to intercept a German high-altitude reconnaissance aircraft over Kaunas, Lithuania at 30,000ft (9,144m). All three aircraft entered irrecoverable spins and the pilots were forced to bail out, one being killed. Investigations found the crew to be inexperienced (it was their first high-altitude sortie) and problems with pumps resulted in insufficient fuel and oil pressure at altitude.

The MiG-3 was optimised as a high-altitude fighter and above 20,000ft (6,096m) its 356kts (398mph) top speed bettered that of the German Bf 109E (331kts/382mph). However, at lower altitudes the MiG's advantage

The modified aircraft first flew on October 29, 1940 and was initially classified as the fourth prototype I-200/MiG-1, but it was so significantly different to the earlier design that it was dubbed the MiG-3 after passing State acceptance trials in December.
MiGAvia/Russian Aircraft Corporation

The MiG-1's lateral stability was improved in the MiG-3 by increasing the dihedral on the outer wing panels by a further one degree and the engine was moved forwards by 4in to improve longitudinal stability. This increased the length of the fuselage and the designers found that if a new water radiator was also fitted, enough room was created to allow an additional 55 Imp Gal fuel tank to be fitted beneath the pilot's seat and an extra oil tank to be mounted below the engine.

The MiG-3 was optimised as a high-altitude fighter and above 20,000ft its top speed bettered that of the German Bf 109E. However, at lower altitudes the MiG's advantage disappeared as its maximum speed at sea level was almost identical to the Messerschmitt. The MiG's manoeuvrability was inferior to the Messerschmitt's because of its higher wing loading and the increased weight compared to the MiG-1 resulted in a poor climb rate.

> ### MiG-4 & MiG-6 'Shturmoviks'
> One of the earliest MiG designs was the stillborn MiG-4 and MiG-6 projects. The basic concept had been underway before Mikoyan and Gurevich left Polikarpov, where they had been part of a programme named Project 65. This used the same Mikulin engine as the I-200 fighter design but employed it in ground attack aircraft named the PBSh-1 and PBSh-2.
>
> The design requirement called for extensive use of armour plate and the PBSh-1 (later referred to as the MiG-4) used this to form part of the structural design. The aircraft had a projected top speed of 253kts (292mph) and was to be equipped with two cannons and six machine guns. The sister PBSh-2 (later to become the MiG-6 project) used the same AM-38 engine and fuselage but employed a unique reverse sesquiplane wing arrangement, with the upper wing being smaller than the lower. Both wings were also to be forward swept.
>
> Work on both projects was underway when the ruling party ordered it to cease. It later transpired that Ilyushin's BSh-2 had received the contract and went into production as the Il-2 Shturmovik. In combination with its successor, the Ilyushin Il-10, a total of 42,330 were built, making it the single most produced military aircraft design in aviation history. Conversely, neither the MiG-4 nor the MiG-6 would ever leave the drawing board.

disappeared as its maximum speed at sea level was almost identical to the German's at only 278kts (314 mph).

The MiG's manoeuvrability was inferior to the Messerschmitt's because of its higher wing loading and the increased weight compared to the MiG-1 resulted in a poor climb rate. This lack of performance was exacerbated by the MiG-3's instability at high speeds, which made it a poor gunnery platform as it had a tendency to 'wander' and needed constant pilot input to remain on target.

The MiG's weaponry was also lacking compared to its German foe. The standard armament consisted of one 0.50in (12.7mm) UBS machine gun and two 0.30in (7.62mm) ShKAS machine guns, all mounted in the engine cowling and synchronised to fire through the propeller arc. Meanwhile, the Bf 109 it mostly encountered had a single 0.79in (20mm) cannon and two 0.31in (7.92mm) machine guns.

From mid-1941 the first of 821 MiG-3s were delivered with a single 0.50in (12.7mm) UBK machine gun in a pod under each wing. This reduced the fighter's speed by about 10kts (12mph) at all altitudes – something which resulted in a number of pilots removing the pods.

Other airframes were modified with a pair of UBS machine guns in place of the ShKAS weapons and a further 215 machines were fitted out to carry six RS-82 rockets. A total of 72 MiG-3s were also fitted with a pair of 0.79in (20mm) ShVAK cannons.

In Regiment use a whole gamut of armament options were trialled at the request of frustrated pilots but the MiG-3 always remained woefully under-armed. To make matters worse the various weapons proved to be very unreliable and the gunsights were so inaccurate that pilots resorted to getting as close to their enemy as possible and firing at point black range!

PRODUCTION TERMINATED
Whereas just 100 MiG-1s had been produced, its successor was to serve in vast numbers. On December 9, 1940, the People's Ministry of the Aircraft Industry announced that Zavod No 1 would be required to build a total of 3,500 MiG-3s in 1941 and Zavod No 43 in Kiev would also begin construction of the type.

The year got off to a good start with 140 aircraft delivered in January. During 1941, 25 MiG-3 were produced per day and by the beginning of the Great Patriotic War (June 22, 1941), the MiGs had become the most numerous type of fighter aircraft in the Soviet Air Force – in fact 89.9% of all new fighters serving with the VVS were MiG-3s.

However, by October the German advance on Moscow forced the Mikoyan-Gurevich Design Bureau and its factory to evacuate 550 miles (885km) east to Kuybyshev where work resumed under harsh and inhospitable conditions.

Machinery had been moved in such a fashion that it would be possible to start producing new MiG-3s within days of opening the new factory; the first few being assembled from pre-finished parts prepared at the Moscow factory. Full production was just in the process of beginning again when Stalin ordered assembly of the MiG-3 to effectively be terminated in favour of the Ilyushin Il-2 Shturmovik. The MiG's poor reputation

Left: By June 1941, MiGs had become the most numerous type of fighter aircraft of the new generation in the Soviet Air Force – in fact 89.9% of all new fighters serving with the VVS were MiG-3s. They did not fare well. **Right:** The MiG-3s were among the best fighters available to Russian pilots during Operation *Barbarossa*, but they proved mostly unsuitable for the battle in hand. The MiG had been designed primarily as a high-altitude interceptor fighter but over the Eastern Front crews found themselves tangling with combat-experienced German pilots at lower altitudes.

Left: Aleksandr Pokryshkin finished the war with 53 official air combat victories, a number of which were achieved while flying a MiG-3 at the beginning of the war. **Right:** A VVS MiG-3 is readied for flight during the summer of 1941.

with its pilots had finally filtered through to bureaucratic circles and this, combined with the cancellation of the AM-35A engine programme led to the aircraft's eventual demise.

No entirely new MiG-3s would be made at Kuybyshev but 35 airframes were produced from spare parts in 1942. These final assemblies infuriated Stalin, who wanted the Il-2 to be built at Kuybyshev in as large a number as possible. On December 23, he sent a telegram to the factory directors, Shenkman and Tretyakov, stating: *"You have deceived our country and our Red Army. Our Red Army needs Il-2s now as much as it needs bread and water. Shenkman is producing one Il-2 per day and Tretyakov is producing one to two MiG-3s. This is an insult to the country and the Red Army. We need Il-2s, not MiGs. This is your final warning."* Days later the production of Il-2s had surpassed even Stalin's wildest expectations.

OPERATION *BARBAROSSA*
The first MiG-3s were delivered to frontline regiments from the early spring of 1941 but quickly proved to be a handful for pilots more accustomed to the docile and lower-performance Polikarpov biplanes. Even those who had flown the Polikarpov I-16 monoplane found the slippery MiG monoplane a handful.

With German invasion looking ever more likely, Russia found itself in a strange situation where it had far more MiG-3s than it had pilots able to fly them. By the beginning of June 1941, a total of 1,029 aircraft had been delivered but just 494 pilots had been signed off as competent to handle the new fighters.

"We need Il-2s, not MiGs. This is your final warning" – Stalin

Nevertheless, the first German aircraft to fall to the guns of the MiG-3 came before the official invasion, when pilots from the 4th Fighter Regiment shot down three German Junkers Ju-86P high-altitude reconnaissance aircraft in early June. However high-altitude combat of this sort was to prove uncommon on the Eastern Front when the war started for real.

When Operation *Barbarossa*, the German invasion of Russia, began on June 22, 1941, MiG-3s were in service with the VVS, PVO and Soviet Naval Aviation. Most of the aircraft were based in the border military districts of the Soviet Union with 164 examples in the Leningrad Military District, 135 in the Baltic Military District, 233 in the Western Special Military District, 190 in the Kiev Military District and 195 in the Odessa Military District. However, a large number of these aircraft were already unserviceable before the German invasion began.

The first aircraft to fall to the guns of a MiG-3 during Operation *Barbarossa* was a Romanian Bristol Blenheim reconnaissance bomber shot down by a pilot from the 4th Fighter Regiment assigned to the Odessa Military District.

The MiG-3s were among the best fighters available to Russian pilots, but they proved mostly unsuitable for the battle in hand. The MiG had been designed primarily as a high-altitude interceptor fighter but over the Eastern Front crews found themselves tangling with combat-experienced German pilots at lower altitudes – typically well below 16,000ft (4,877m).

The MiG-3 was difficult to fly in peacetime and much more so in combat, especially at low-level where its turning

Left: The MiG-3 was a fast aeroplane but lacked stability and as such was a poor gun platform. **Right:** When it became apparent that the MiG-3 was outdated and underperforming compared to the German aircraft of the day, a number of attempts were made to upgrade it. The aircraft had originally been designed around the Mikulin AM-37 but MiG had resorted to the lower-powered AM-35 due to necessity. With the AM-37 now reaching maturity, the opportunity was taken to install an example in a MiG-3 in May 1941 for evaluation purposes. Dubbed the MiG-7 the aircraft and engine combination proved to be even worse than the MiG-3. The following month's invasion by Germany caused the cancellation of both the AM-37 and the MiG-7.

capabilities were limited and its instability an ever-present danger. It was not uncommon for MiGs being pursued by German Messerschmitt Bf 109s to fly, stall, flick or spin into the ground without actually needing to be shot down by the enemy.

It soon became apparent that not only was the MiG-3 inferior to German fighters but it was also being outperformed by contemporary Russian aircraft such as the Yakovlev Yak-1. As its unsuitability for air-to-air combat became apparent, many MiG-3s were relegated to the PVO, where their problems mattered less – or were reassigned to ground attack/fighter bomber roles, for which they were equally unsuited.

By October, when the German offensive towards Moscow (codenamed Operation *Typhoon*) began, just 257 MiG-3s remained assigned to VVS fighter units – despite more than 1,000 new aircraft being delivered since the start of the German invasion.

SOVIET ACE

Setting aside the MiG-3's aforementioned limitations, some were flown to great success by the most talented of Russian pilots. These included Aleksandr Pokryshkin, who finished the war with 53 official air combat victories, a number of which were achieved while flying a MiG-3 at the beginning of the war.

Pokryshkin was stationed in Moldavia in June 1941 flying MiG-3s and his airfield was bombed on the first day of the war. His first 'victory' was actually a disaster when he shot down an aircraft that he had seen and not recognised. It turned out to be a Soviet Sukhoi Su-2 bomber, which was so top secret that even Soviet pilots had not been told about it! It was only when the aircraft dived away trailing flame that Pokryshkin noticed the red stars

> **"Machine gun pods reduced the fighter's speed by about 10kts"**

on the wings. The pilot, M I Gudzenko (squadron commander of the 211th Bomber Aviation Regiment), escaped unharmed, but his gunner was killed. Flying in front of other MiG-3 pilots who were lining up on the Sukhoi bombers, Pokryshkin was able to prevent an even greater disaster.

The following day he claimed a Bf 109 downed after he and his wingman were 'bounced' by five enemy fighters during a reconnaissance mission. His victories continued to rise and in the autumn of 1941 Pokryshkin, flying a MiG-3, took off in sleet to single-handedly locate the 1st Panzer Group, a mission for which he was awarded the Order of Lenin.

Pokryshkin flew the MiG-3 until the summer of 1942 when he moved initially onto the Yak-1 and then onto the Bell P-39 Airacobra. He later recalled: "The operational advantage of the MiG-3 seemed to be obscured by its certain defects. However, these advantages could undoubtedly be exploited by a pilot able to discover them."

MiG-7 & MiG-9

When it became apparent that the MiG-3 was outdated and underperforming compared to the German aircraft of the day, a number of attempts were made to upgrade it.

The aircraft had originally been designed around the Mikulin AM-37 but had resorted to the lower-powered AM-35 due to necessity. With the AM-37 now reaching maturity, the opportunity was taken to install an example in a MiG-3 in May 1941 for evaluation purposes.

Dubbed the MiG-7 the aircraft and engine combination proved to be even worse than the MiG-3. The airframe had poor longitudinal stability and the powerplant itself still had a number of significant problems and the following month's invasion by Germany caused the

Left: Another MiG-3 was modified to accommodate the Shvetsov ASh-82A radial engine, which was then entering production. It was hoped this would improve the aircraft's performance at low altitude but the resulting I-210 prototype (also known as the MiG-3-82) failed to deliver. **Right:** The MiG I-211 was also known as the MiG-9M-82 and used the same Shvetsov ASh-82A radial engine as the MiG-3-82. The aircraft flew for the first time during January 1942 but test pilots found the big radial engine's profile produced so much drag that it more than cancelled out any benefits from the engine's extra power. Furthermore, the ASh-82 produced so many fumes that it was impossible to fly the aircraft with the canopy closed for fear of suffocation.

In 1943 MiG received a request from the VVS to develop an improved version of the MiG-3 capable of reaching 362kts at 41,010ft. To be called the I-230 or MiG-3U (Uluchshennyi or Improved), the new aircraft would need a considerable reduction in weight and it was decided this would be achieved by using a fuselage of entirely wooden monocoque construction and covered in plywood skins. The prototype was first flown on May 31, 1943 and a further five examples were built over the next two months. Although the aircraft showed promising performance, the I-230 was never ordered into production.

The OKB began modifying the I-230 in September 1943 by fitting the new 1,800hp AM-39A engine. The new aircraft was designated as the I-231 and was developed as a back-up programme for the I-220. It first flew on October 19, 1943 but the project was completely shelved in May 1944 because of the unreliability of the powerplant. The I-230 would be the last variant of the MiG-3 family.

MiG OKB stuck with the idea of re-engining the MiG-3 with a radial engine and the resulting MiG-9Ye was a direct descendent of the earlier I-210 but used an improved 1,850hp ASh-82F engine. Improvements included aerodynamic refinements of the engine cowling and the cockpit was moved aft by almost 10in. The reduction in drag and weight enabled it to reach 365kts at 23,000ft but by then the Lavochkin La-5 was already in production and as the rival aircraft boasted similar performance the MiG project was cancelled.

cancellation of both the AM-37 and the MiG-7. From now on, Mikulin's resources were required for the AM-35 and AM-38 engines already in production.

A single MiG-3 was also retrofitted with the AM-38 engine from the Ilyushin Il-2 in July 1941. This proved to be 8kts (9mph) faster than the standard MiG at sea level and was also more manoeuvrable, but the engine was prone to overheating in the fighter's slim nose. The variant was recommended for production but the prototype was shot down on October 5 and the project was shelved as the supply of AM-38 engines was felt better suited to Il-2 airframes. Nevertheless, later in the war around 80 MiG-3s were retrofitted with AM-38s in a last-ditch attempt to make them airworthy.

Another MiG-3 was modified to accommodate the Shvetsov ASh-82A radial engine, which was then entering production. It was hoped this would improve the aircraft's performance at low altitude but the resulting I-210 prototype (also known as the MiG-3-82) failed to deliver.

Undeterred, the Russians modified the airframe again, this time to include a much shorter fuselage and a pair of large air ducts atop the round cowling that housed the 49in (126cm) diameter engine. This latest variant was initially referred to as the I-211 but from late December 1941 was re-designated as the MiG-9M-82. The aircraft flew for the first time during January 1942 but test pilots found the big radial engine's profile produced so much drag that it more than cancelled out any benefits from the engine's extra power. In fact, the MiG-9M-82's performance figures were even worse than the standard MiG-3. Furthermore, the ASh-82 produced so many fumes that it was impossible to fly the aircraft with the canopy closed for fear of suffocation.

EXPERIMENTAL BUREAU

Mikoyan and Gurevich were now in a precarious position as a design bureau that wasn't actually designing or producing any of its own aeroplanes. Luckily, Stalin had chosen to designate the company an OKB (experimental design bureau) rather than just a KB (design bureau). This meant it could work on a number of prototypes that would further its aeronautical knowledge without jeopardising any production contracts.

These projects included research into areas such as supercharged engines and pressurised cockpits and in March 1942 Artem Mikoyan was officially named director and chief design engineer of the company.

By April 1942 the Germans had been pushed back from the gates of Moscow and the tide of the war was turning. MiG OKB was able to return to the Russian capital and moved into a new, purpose built, site in the suburbs.

While sorting through the various equipment and components returned to the city, engineers discovered sufficient parts to create 50 new MiG-3 airframes. These were assembled and delivered to the VVS where they were assigned to the defence of Moscow. These final examples took the total MiG-3 production to 3,322 airframes.

Undeterred by the abject failure of the

◀ The MiG I-220 was a far larger aircraft than the MiG-3 from which it was developed. In fact it was a completely new aircraft that shared only its general configuration with the MiG-3. It was a sleek and very aerodynamically clean single-engine fighter with a low wing and retractable taildragger landing gear, with radiators added to the wing centre section. The I-220 was of mixed construction, the fuselage being made of metal forward of the cockpit, the rest being a wooden monocoque, while the wings were spruce skins over metal framework. It was unofficially referred to as the MiG-11.

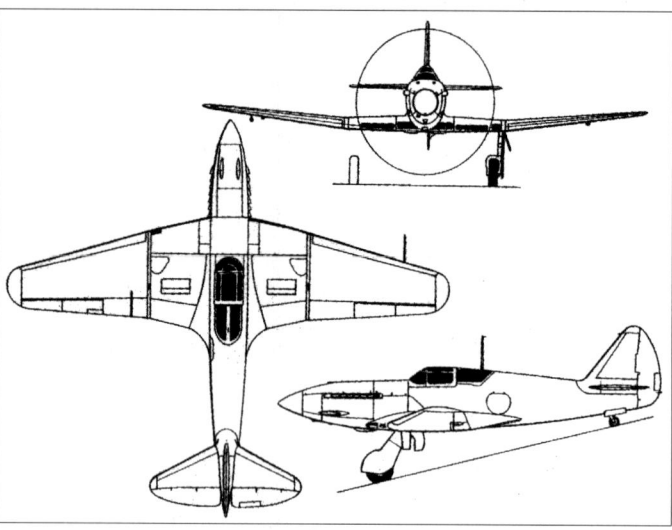

The wing profile on the I-220 and subsequent variants differed greatly from earlier versions of the MiG-3 family.

Research continued into 1944 with the I-222 variant benefiting from an improved turbocharged AM-39B engine, a pressurised cockpit and the fuselage cut down behind the cockpit to improve the view from the rear. It flew on May 7, 1944 and continued in tests until it was retired in July 1945.

I-210 (MiG-9M-82) programme, MiG OKB stuck with the idea of re-engining the MiG-3 with a radial engine. The resulting MiG-9Ye was a direct descendent of the earlier I-210 but used an improved 1,850hp ASh-82F engine. Improvements included aerodynamic refinements of the engine cowling and the cockpit was moved aft by almost 10in (24.5cm). The oil cooler inlets were also moved to the wing roots and a larger tail was fitted to improve stability. The MiG-9Ye weighed 660lbs (300kg) less than its predecessor but these changes took most of 1942 to design and assembly did not begin until December 1942.

The MiG-9Ye first flew on February 24, 1943 and the reduction in drag and weight enabled it to reach 365kts (420mph) at 23,000ft (7,010m). The time to climb to 16,000ft (4,877m) also took just four minutes. MiG OKB had originally planned to build ten in the first quarter of 1943, but trials were not finished until the first quarter of 1944. By then the Lavochkin La-5 was already in production and as the rival aircraft boasted similar performance the MiG project was cancelled.

Two days after the MiG-9Ye performed its maiden flight the MiG OKB received a request from the VVS to develop an improved version of the MiG-3 capable of reaching 362kts (416mph) at 41,010ft (12,500m) and reach 32,800ft (10,000m) in just 13 minutes.

To be called the I-230 or MiG-3U (Uluchshennyi or Improved), the new aircraft would need a considerable reduction in weight and it was decided this would achieved by using a fuselage of entirely wooden monocoque construction and covered in plywood skins. Conversely, the original wooden main spar was replaced by a metal spar. The fuselage was lengthened to improve stability at high altitude and the cockpit was moved back with a raised canopy to improve visibility.

The engine was an AM-35A with 0.732 reduction gear. Built with spare parts from an AM-35A and AM-38 (because of engine shortages), it was 88lbs (40kg) heavier than the standard AM-35A and turned a 10ft 5in (3.20m) diameter propeller.

The prototype was first flown by test

MiG OKB rebuilt the second prototype I-220 with a new turbocharged AM-42B powerplant and a pressurised cockpit. Dubbed the I-225, it also had a cut-down rear fuselage and four cannons. Its first flight was on July 21, 1944 but it was destroyed in August after an engine fire forced the pilot to crash land.

A single I-224 variant was also manufactured – this being almost identical to the I-222 apart from its AM-39FB (with an improved turbocharger) and an oversized four-bladed propeller. The I-224 flew for the first time on September 26, 1944 and was used for evaluation until 1946.

Left: As far back as 1940, while its efforts were mostly employed in the development of the MiG-1 the company was also working on an aircraft to meet a requirement for a twin-engine long-range escort fighter, or Dalniy Istrebitel Soprovozhdenya (DIS). The MiG DIS-200 was of mixed wood and metal construction and was powered by a pair of 1,400hp Mikulin AM-37 water-cooled V-12 engines driving three-bladed propellers. Armament comprised of twin 12.7mm UBS machine guns and four 7.62mm ShKAS machine guns. A single VYa 23mm cannon, torpedo or 2,200lb bomb could also be fitted in a detachable ventral pod. **Right:** The prototype MiG-5 flew for the first time on June 11, 1941 but VVS priority was given to the Petlyakov Pe-3 twin-engined fighter instead. Nonetheless, a second prototype was completed anyway and flew on January 28, 1943. This variant was fitted with 1,700hp Shvetsov M-82 14-cylinder radial engines driving four-bladed propellers and the armament increased to add a second 23mm cannon.

pilot V N Savkin on May 31, 1943 and a further five examples were built over the next two months. The first aircraft's engine had a tendency to overheat and all examples were described as difficult to land. The most evident defect was excessive oil leaking through the coupling of the reduction shaft and the aircraft returned from every flight smeared in lubricant. This was considered unacceptable by test pilots, but it was probably due to the hybrid engines. Although the aircraft showed promising performance, the I-230 was never ordered into production.

Proving it was a company that was difficult to deter, MiG OKB began modifying the I-230 in September 1943 by fitting the new 1,800hp AM-39A engine. The new aircraft was designated as the I-231 and it was developed alongside a separate new high-altitude fighter referred to as the I-220. Both aircraft used the same AM-39A variant powerplant although the I-220 was a far larger aircraft than the I-230 and the MiG-3 from which it was developed. The I-231 was actually developed as a back-up programme for the I-220 and first flew on October 19, 1943.

Following an engine failure the aircraft was returned to the air and achieved a top speed of 382kts (439mph) at 23,294ft (7,100m). The aircraft could also reach 16,404ft (5,000m) in 4.5 minutes. This made it the best performing piston-powered Soviet fighter to date but the project was completely shelved in May 1944 because of the unreliability of the powerplant. The I-230 would be the last variant of the MiG-3 family.

> "It was impossible to fly the ASh-82A-engined MiG with the canopy closed for fear of suffocation"

HIGH ALTITUDE FIGHTER

The I-220 itself was a completely new aircraft that shared only its general configuration with the MiG-3. It was a sleek and very aerodynamically clean single-engine fighter with a low wing and retractable taildragger landing gear, with radiators fitted into the wing centre section. The I-220 was of mixed construction, the fuselage being made of metal forward of the cockpit, the rest being a wooden monocoque, while the wings were spruce skins over metal framework. The cockpit was unpressurised; the canopy sliding back to open.

The prototype was powered by a low-altitude Mikulin AM-38F engine providing 1,700hp of thrust and was and armed with twin 20mm ShVAK cannons above the engine, firing through the propeller arc.

The AM-38F engine limited the prototype's ceiling to 31,200ft (9,500m) but performance proved excellent, suggesting the design had great promise. The I-220 was then re-engined with a 1,800hp Mikulin AM-39 giving it improved high-altitude performance, with flights beginning in May 1943.

A second I-220 prototype was fitted from the outset with the AM-39 and four 20mm ShVAK cannons, the additional armament being mounted in the lower part of the nose and also firing through the propeller arc. This second prototype first flew in early 1944, but by that time MiG OKB engineers had decided that the I-220 would not be able to achieve its ceiling specification, and the design needed to be rethought.

As such, the second prototype was rebuilt as the I-221 with a 42ft 7in (12.97m) long-span wing and an AM-39A engine fitted with twin turbochargers. The variant flew on December 2, 1943, with test

The MiG-8 Utka started life in 1945 as a demonstrator to test out the canard aircraft configuration for potential jet fighter designs. However, rather than modify an existing single-seat aircraft, MiG OKB engineers designed the aircraft as a three-seat sport machine. The MiG-8's performance turned out to be good for its class, and its 'spin-proof' handling was excellent. It also promised to be cheap to manufacture but sadly MiG OKB couldn't interest anyone in putting the Utka into production.

Perhaps one of the most unusual MiG aircraft of all time was the I-250, which would evolve into the MiG-13. This distinctive aircraft featured an air reaction engine compressor which drove both a combustion chamber and a conventional propeller. The first of two prototypes took to the air on April 4, 1945 but the project was beset with problems and it was cancelled in November 1946 after MiG officials were sacked and then arrested for 'sabotage.'

pilot P A Zhuravlyov at the controls, but it only completed eight flights before being lost on February 7, 1944. Investigation showed that the pilot had seen flames from the turbocharger system and, finding the cockpit filling up with smoke, had assumed the aircraft was on fire; he decided to bail out.

By that time, German high-altitude reconnaissance overflights were generally a thing of the past, and there was no real need for a high-altitude fighter. However, research continued and engineers produced a single I-222, which was based on the I-221 but had an improved turbocharged AM-39B engine, a pressurised cockpit, and the fuselage cut down behind the cockpit to improve the view from the rear. It flew on May 7, 1944 and continued in tests until it was retired in July 1945.

Sometime later MiG OKB rebuilt the second prototype I-220 with a new turbocharged AM-42B powerplant and a pressurised cockpit. Dubbed the I-225, it also had a cut-down rear fuselage and four cannons. Its first flight was on July 21, 1944, with Aleksei Yakimov at the controls. The aircraft was lost after an engine fire on August 9 and although Yakimov survived he suffered burns.

A second I-225 prototype was built, performing its maiden flight on March 14, 1945, with Aleksandr Deyev at the helm. It was badly damaged in a take-off accident on April 16, but was rebuilt and continued as a test aircraft until March 1947 when it was finally retired.

A single I-224 variant was also manufactured – this being almost identical to the I-222 apart from its AM-39FB (with an improved turbocharger) and an oversized four-bladed propeller. The I-224 flew for the first time on September 26, 1944 and was used for evaluation until 1946.

TWIN MiG-5

Mention of the piston-powered family of MiG aircraft could not be complete without discussion of the sole multi-engined piston-powered fighter to emerge from the design bureau.

As far back as 1940, while its efforts were mostly employed in the development of the MiG-1 the company was also working on an aircraft to meet a requirement for a twin-engine long-range escort fighter, or Dalniy Istrebitel Soprovozhdenya (DIS).

The need came after Soviet officials witnessed the success of the Messerschmitt Me 110 during the Battle of Britain and MiG OKB submitted a design it dubbed the DIS-200 or MiG-5. The company was surprised to meet stiff competition from aircraft as diverse as the Grushin Gr-1, the Polikarpov TIS and the Tairov Ta-3.

The MiG DIS-200 was of mixed wood and metal construction and was powered by a pair of 1,400hp Mikulin AM-37 water-cooled V-12 engines driving three-bladed propellers. Armament comprised of twin 12.7mm UBS machine guns and four 7.62mm ShKAS machine guns. A single VYa 23mm cannon, torpedo or 2,200lb bomb could also be fitted in a detachable ventral pod.

> " The prototype MiG-5's nose was partially glazed on the bottom to allow the pilot to see below "

The attractive tailwheel aircraft had wings that were of an 'inverted gull' configuration and had a leading edge that almost merged into the machine's nose. At the rear were a pair of stylish twin fins. The cockpit itself afforded an excellent view and the nose was also partially glazed on the bottom to allow the pilot to see below.

The prototype MiG-5 flew for the first time on June 11, 1941 with Aleksandr I Zhukov at the controls. A dedicated bomber version (referred to tentatively as the MiG-2) was also considered but trials showed the aircraft was incapable of meeting the required performance specifications and further work was abandoned. VVS priority was given to the Petlyakov Pe-3 twin-engined fighter instead. The country needed weapons immediately and there was no great point in trying to get the MiG-5 up to a standard that the Pe-3 could already meet.

Nonetheless, a second prototype was completed anyway and flew on January 28, 1943. This variant was fitted with 1,700hp Shvetsov M-82 14-cylinder radial engines driving four-bladed propellers and the armament increased to add a second 23mm cannon. It also included a tailcone that could split open to act as an airbrake. Performance was still lacking however and the programme was soon cancelled completely.

MiG-8 – THE CIVIL DUCK

Although MiG has most notably made its name as a manufacturer of military aircraft, one of its more unusual offerings was a civilian light aircraft.

The aircraft started life in 1945 as a demonstrator to test out the canard aircraft configuration (which has a foreplane in front of the main wing instead of a tailplane) for potential jet fighter designs. However, rather than modify an existing single-seat aircraft, MiG OKB engineers designed the MiG-8 as a three-seat sport aircraft. It was named Utka (Duck), since 'canard' is actually French for 'duck.'

The MiG-8 performed its first flight late in 1945, with Aleksei N Grinchik at the controls. It was of wood and fabric construction, with a high-mounted strut-braced swept wing in the rear and a tailplane on a slender extended nose that suggested a duck's bill. There were twin triangular tailfins, originally mounted on the wingtips, then moved into midwing; and the wings had fixed slats on the front of the outer sections of the span.

The Utka had fixed tricycle landing gear and all of the wheels were covered with spats. The powerplant was a 110hp five-cylinder Shvetsov M-11FM air-cooled radial engine which drove a two-bladed fixed-pitch wooden propeller mounted in pusher configuration on the rear. The pilot sat at the front of the aircraft with two passenger seats in parallel behind.

The MiG-8's performance turned out to be good for its class, and its 'spin-proof' handling was excellent. It also promised to be cheap to manufacture but sadly MiG OKB couldn't interest anyone in putting the Utka into production.

MiG-13 HYBRID FIGHTER

Perhaps one of the most unusual MiG aircraft of all time was the I-250, which would evolve into the MiG-13.

This distinctive aircraft featured the Vozdushno-Reactivny Dvigatel Kompressomiy (VRDK or air reaction engine compressor), which was developed by Soviet engine designer Konstantin Kholshchevnikov in 1942. This powerplant involved a turbojet engine of sorts, with a compressor feeding a combustion chamber, but the compressor stage was driven by a piston engine, which also drove a conventional propeller.

MiG OKB began work on the I-250, which was to be powered by the VRDK and a Klimov VK-107R piston engine, in early 1944 and the first of two prototypes took to the air on April 4, 1945 with test pilot Aleksandr P Deyev at the controls.

Initial flights were conducted with just the Klimov piston engine in place – as the VRDK was not ready – and even when it did, it suffered substantial teething problems. The second prototype flew in May 1945 and still the aircraft would take-off and fly with only the piston engine, engaging the VRDK only when boost power was needed. With the unit employed the aircraft could easily exceed 435kts (500mph) at altitude.

The programme suffered a setback on July 5, 1945 when the first prototype crashed, killing Deyev. The crash was due to a structural failure, not an engine problem but was a blow to the entire MiG OKB team.

Nevertheless the VVS ordered ten pre-production machines. Even though the aircraft didn't seem to promise much as a frontline fighter it was thought it could be useful for conversion training on to conventional jet aircraft.

Once again, things did not go smoothly with the programme encountering problems that saw officials sacked and then arrested for 'sabotage.' At a meeting on November 29, 1946 chaired by Josef Stalin himself, the decision was made to not put the MiG-13 into production. Pure jet aircraft were now being seen as much more promising… and MiG was to seize this new challenge with typical enthusiasm and aplomb. ❖

SPECIFICATION MIKOYAN-GUREVICH MiG-3

Crew	1
Length	27ft 1in (8.25m)
Wingspan	33ft 5in (10.20m)
Height	10ft 10in (3.30m)
Wing Area	188ft² (17.44 m²)
Empty Weight	5,965lbs (2,699kg)
Loaded Weight	7,415lbs (3,355kg)
Max Speed	(Sea Level) 273kts (313mph/505km/h)
Max Speed	at 25,000ft 346kts (398mph/640km/h)
Service Ceiling	39,400ft (12,000m)
Combat Range	510 miles (820km)
Powerplant:	One 1,350hp Mikulin AM-35A liquid-cooled V12 engine

Armament
One 12.7 mm Berezin UB machine gun, two 7.62 mm ShKAS machine guns in the cowl, six RS-82 rockets or two 220lb (100kg) bombs

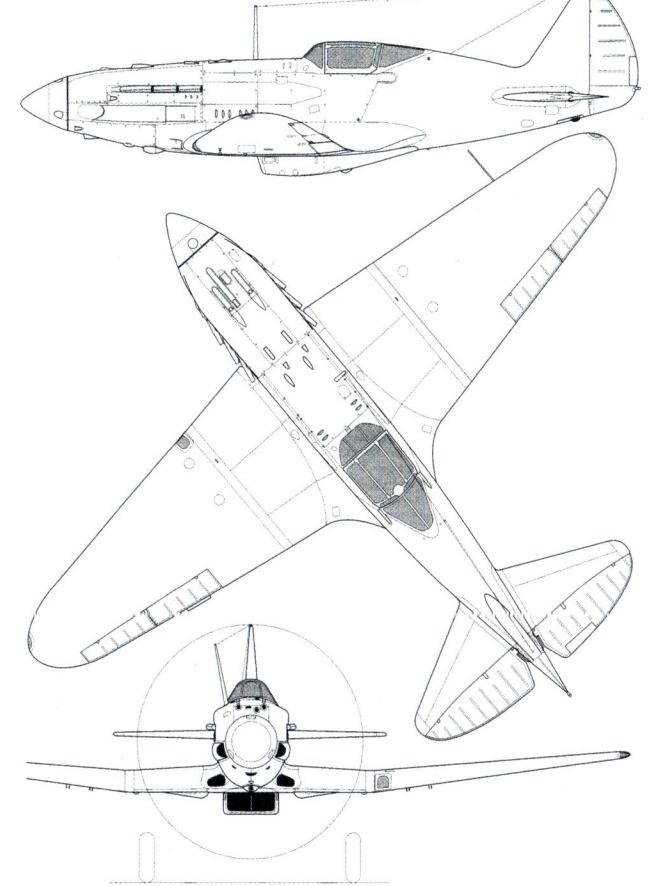

Key Publishing – Pete West

Red 01 (c/n 114010) is one of just four MiG-9s thought to exist today. It is on display at the Central Air Force Museum in Monino near Moscow. *Steve Bridgewater*

MiG Enters the Jet Age

With Britain, Germany and the USA all having jet fighters by the end of World War Two, it was inevitable that the USSR would follow suit – and once again the MiG OKB was at the forefront of development. Steve Bridgewater investigates the history of the MiG-9 *Fargo*

The advent of the turbojet engine in Germany and Britain in the mid-1930s eventually led to a flurry of jet-powered fighter aircraft.

Frank Whittle patented a design for an engine featuring a two-stage axial compressor feeding a single-sided centrifugal compressor in January 1930 and his first engine ran in April 1937.

Meanwhile, Hans von Ohain patented a similar engine in Germany in 1935 and experienced far greater support from his nation's leaders. As such, the Heinkel He 178 became the world's first aircraft to fly under turbojet power on August 27, 1939.

Whittle, on the other hand, was unable to interest the government in his invention, and development continued at a slow pace. The Gloster E.28/39 was therefore the first British jet-engined aircraft to fly, but not until May 15, 1941.

Both the He 178 and E.28/39 were merely test aircraft and it would fall to the Messerschmitt Me 262 to launch the jet fighter concept on the world. The German aircraft flew in July 1942 but would not be introduced to operational service until April 1944. In Britain, the Gloster Meteor would fly on March 3, 1943 and entered RAF frontline service on July 27, 1944.

On October 1, 1942, the Bell P-59 Airacomet became the first American jet to fly but the aircraft was only built in small numbers and no American jets entered combat before the war ended.

In Russia, thoughts turned to jet technology in February 1944 when the State Defence Committee established a scientific research institute, the Nauchnyy-Issledovatel'skiy Institut (NII) to gather together all the design teams that had been working on the new engines.

In May, the teams were summoned to a meeting where a programme was created to produce a 'jet air force' for the USSR. Engine development was entrusted to Arkhip Lyulka and V V Uvarov while the aircraft they would power would come from the design bureaus of Lavochkin, Mikoyan-Gurevich, Sukhoi and Yakovlev.

RISING TENSIONS

However, progress was slow and it was only following the 'outbreak of peace' in 1945 that the USSR (and its new American rivals) really started to take the creation of jet fighters seriously. With tensions rising between the two nations it was inevitable that the arms race would advance the development of jet technology exponentially.

Work on the USSR's first jet fighter had actually begun in February 1945 when the Council of People's Commissars ordered Mikoyan-Gurevich and Sukhoi to develop a single-seat jet fighter to be equipped with

The MiG I-270 came about in response to a Soviet Air Force requirement for a rocket-powered interceptor aircraft for use in the point-defence role.

MiG already had experience producing the I-250 (MiG-13) mixed power interceptor, which combined an air reaction compressor motorjet powered by a Klimov VK-107 V12 piston engine. While quite successful when it worked, giving a maximum speed of 443kts (510 mph), problems with the motorjet delayed the programme and it was cancelled in 1948.

two captured German BMW 003 engines.

The BMW 003 was used in both the Heinkel He 162 and the four-engined versions of the Arado Blitz (the Ar 234C), but Soviet forces had seized blueprints for these powerplants from the Basdorf-Zühlsdorf plant near Berlin and the Central Works near Nordhausen.

MiG already had experience producing the I-250 (MiG-13) mixed power interceptor (see page 17) and was also working on the rocket-powered I-270 concept in 1945.

The I-270 came about in response to a Soviet Air Force requirement for a rocket-powered interceptor aircraft for use in the point-defence role. Its configuration was related to the Korolyov RP-318 rocket-powered demonstrator, which first flew February 20, 1940, and the more recent Bereznyak-Isayev BI-1.

MiG's aircraft shared much of the BI-1's design, including its tapered fuselage with a prominent bubble canopy, the straight wing and dual-chambered bipropellant rocket motor. However, it was much larger than the BI-1 and had reinforced wings and a raised T-tail.

The I-270 is also thought to have benefited from captured German technology, specifically from the rocket-powered Me 263 – which was a scaled-up and improved Me 163 Komet with a throttle-able rocket motor. The German prototypes never flew under rocket power and in April 1945 the factory was overrun by American and Russian troops who divided up the assets between themselves.

The I-270 began glide testing in December 1945 – towed aloft behind a Tupolev Tu-2 – and the second prototype began powered tests early the following year, but was damaged beyond repair during a hard landing. By this stage,

According to the Council of People's Commissars requirement, MiG's I-300 was to be armed with a 2.2in (57m) NL-57 cannon mounted in the centreline engine intake bulkhead as well as a pair of 0.9in (23mm) Nudelman-Suranov NS-23 autocannons mounted below the air intakes. The N-57 was provided with 28 rounds and the two NS-23 cannons had 80 rounds each.

turbojet technology was at a far more advanced stage than it had been at the outset of the project, and the VVS decided to cancel the rocket-interceptor project.

"The two test pilots tossed a coin to decide which would fly first"

I-300

This cancellation enabled MiG to concentrate fully on the requirement to develop a fighter based around the captured BMW jet engines.

Russian designers had been working on the I-300 concept alongside the I-270 and, in accordance with the Council of People's Commissars requirement, it was created as a single-seat jet fighter intended to destroy bombers. As such it was armed with a 2.2in (57mm) NL-57 cannon mounted in the centreline engine intake bulkhead as well as a pair of 0.9in (23mm) Nudelman-Suranov NS-23 autocannons mounted below the air intakes. The N-57 was provided with 28 rounds and the two NS-23 cannons had 80 rounds each.

The order also stipulated that the aircraft be capable of 486kts (559mph) at sea level and 491kts (565mph) at 16,400ft (5,000m). Furthermore, it needed to reach that altitude in less than four minutes and should have a range of 510 miles (820km).

In order to improve airflow to the engines during take-off the I-300 was fitted with tricycle landing gear (ensuring the nose was kept lower than a tailwheel configuration) and in a break from the norm the new MiG was to be of all metal construction. The un-swept wing was mid-mounted and fitted with both slotted flaps and Frise type ailerons.

Three prototypes of the I-300 were ordered to be ready for flight tests by March 15, 1946.

For its new fighter, the MiG OKB chose a pod and single boom layout. This enabled the designers to keep the jet pipes as short as possible (to minimise loss of efficiency) and also protected the rear fuselage from the hot jet exhausts. The engines themselves were fitted behind the unpressurised cockpit in the lower fuselage and a steel laminate heatshield was installed on the bottom of the rear fuselage to further protect it from the exhaust gasses.

In order to improve airflow to the engines during take-off, the I-300 was fitted with tricycle landing gear (ensuring the nose was kept lower than a tailwheel configuration) and in a break from the norm the new MiG was to be of all metal construction. The un-swept wing was mid-mounted and fitted with both slotted flaps and Frise-type ailerons.

FLIPPING A COIN

By the time the prototype was ready for assembly Soviet engineers had manufactured their own version of the captured BMW 003 engine – dubbed the RD-20 and producing 1,754lb/thrust – and two of these were fitted to the aircraft ahead of ground testing, which began on December 30, 1945.

" Pilots found the MiG-9 simple and enjoyable to fly "

These tests resulted in a number of problems – most notably that the heatshield caused the underside of the rear fuselage to deform because the steel and the duralumin skin of the fuselage had different expansion ratios when heated. Both the fuselage and heatshield were therefore redesigned ahead of the maiden flight from Ramenskoye airfield on April 24, 1946.

The Yakovlev OKB had also brought its jet prototype (the Yak-15) to Ramenskoye and legend has it that the two test pilots tossed a coin to decide which would fly first – MiG won and the I-300 took to the skies with Aleksey Grinchik at the controls for a 20-minute flight, becoming the USSR's first jet to fly. Three hours later Mikhail Ivanov took the Yak-15 aloft for an equally successful maiden flight.

Testing showed even more problems with the heatshield, which would deform in flight and cause vibrations. The issue had yet to be resolved when the prototype crashed on July 11 killing Grinchik, who was demonstrating it to a number of high-ranking officials. The accident was attributed to vibration causing an aileron to become detached and strike the tail.

The remaining two prototypes were modified with new heatshields before they started test flying in October and the type began State acceptance trials on December 17, 1946. During the trials the

◄ The MiG-9's engines were fitted behind the unpressurised cockpit in the lower fuselage. This example is receiving maintenance in the open on an airfield.

Yakovlev also brought its Yak-15 jet prototype to Ramenskoye for testing. Three hours after the MiG-9 flew, Mikhail Ivanov took the Yak-15 aloft for an equally successful maiden flight.

Legend has it that the MiG and Yakovlev test pilots tossed a coin to decide which would fly first – MiG won and the I-300 took to the skies with Aleksey Grinchik at the controls for a 20-minute flight, becoming the USSR's first jet to fly.

Left: The MiG-9M was fitted with RD-21 engines and a pressurised cockpit was completed in June 1947. Armament was also rearranged in an attempt to eliminate the gas ingestion problem with the N-37 cannon moved to the underside of the fuselage and the NS-23 guns shifted to the side of the fuselage. This caused the cockpit to be moved forward slightly which gave the pilot a better view when landing. The jet failed its state acceptance tests due to a tendency for the engines to flame out at low rpm. The aircraft was also inferior to the MiG-15, which was already in flight testing. **Right:** The two-seat MiG-9UTI failed to deliver and the type was cancelled after just two prototypes were built.

second prototype's horizontal stabiliser disintegrated during flight, but fortunately the pilot was able to land safely. The same thing later happened to the third prototype in February 1947 and the tail was subsequently redesigned.

MIG-9 *FARGO*

Despite these setbacks the VVS ordered a batch of ten aircraft before its acceptance trials had been completed. The production aircraft was dubbed the I-310 by the manufacturer but entered service with the military as the MiG-9. NATO subsequently gave it the reporting name *Fargo*.

These first ten MiG-9s were actually powered by captured BMW 003 powerplants and were manufactured at Factory No 1 in Kazan. The reason for the hasty order was for the type to take part take part in the November 7, 1946 flypast to commemorate the anniversary of the October Revolution; however poor weather forced the cancellation of the event and two of the jets were sent to join the trials programme while the others were retained by MiG OKB as test-beds.

Test flying showed the MiG-9 generally met the performance requirements stipulated by the Council of People's Commissars and pilots found the jet simple and enjoyable to fly. However, the engine had a tendency to flame out when the nose-mounted cannon was fired at high-altitude (caused by the engine ingesting the gun's gases). Other deficiencies noted by test pilots included the lack of an ejection seat, air brakes, a fire suppression system, self-sealing fuel tanks and cockpit armour.

Despite these factors Artem Mikoyan and Mikhail Gurevich were awarded the Stalin Prize in 1947 in recognition of their achievement and the MiG-9 was ordered into production in December 1946. The state called for 40 single-seaters and ten two-seat trainer variants to be ready to take part in the 1947 May Day parade flypast over Moscow.

As it happened, despite just five months' notice, large numbers of MiG-9s were actually ready for the flypast and these joined with Yak-15s in a mass formation over Red Square. Later in the year, during a Soviet Aviation Day demonstration on August 3, MiG-9s took part in mock dogfights against Tupolev Tu-2 bombers.

TWO-SEATER

The two-seat MiG-9UTI (referred to internally at MiG as the I-301T) was quickly developed and the prototype was based on one of the first batch of ten MiG-9s built for the cancelled 1946 flypast. Dual controls were fitted as was an intercom to allow the instructor and student to communicate in the air. Fuel capacity was reduced by one third to make room for the tandem cockpit and the MiG-9UTI was fitted with ejection seats – based on those used in the German Heinkel He 162 fighter. The prototype was delivered on January 17, 1947 but it was rejected following State acceptance trials that revealed dangerously poor visibility from the rear cockpit.

A second example was delivered in July with greatly improved visibility. The rear cockpit's bulletproof windscreen was now replaced with a larger glass plate and the canopy side panels were also modified. The partition between the two cockpits was also removed and, to improve endurance, two 57 Imp Gal (260 lit) drop tanks were hung below the wings. The new version was also fitted with wing-

An unusual sub-variant of the aircraft was the MiG-9L, a 1949 conversion of a single example to test avionics for the KS-1 Kometa air-launched anti-shipping cruise missile. Changes saw a radome installed in the nose for a radar transmitter, a small pod with a radar receiver fitted to the leading inboard edge of each wing and a blister was added to the top of the tailfin to house the missile's radio control system. Finally, a second cockpit with a small bubble canopy was fitted in the middle of the aircraft's back for a flight engineer.

Left: The two-seat MiG-9 introduced wingtip-mounted fuel tanks and these were also used on the later MiG-9M. **Right:** Attempts to remedy the engine stalling problems caused by the intake-mounted cannon were never really successful. Two aircraft were fitted with a rectangular vane on the barrel of the N-37 cannon that dispersed the airflow from the weapon and allowed all three guns to be fired simultaneously. However, the vane affected the aircraft's directional stability and caused it to yaw after just five shots. Worse still, the vane was found to disintegrate after around 800 shots had been fired. *MiGAvia/Russian Aircraft Corporation*

mounted air brakes and it easily passed its acceptance trials late in 1947. However, by this time the entire MiG-9 programme was deemed obsolete and the MiG-9UTI was the first variant to be cancelled. Just two examples had been built.

MODIFIED MiGs
The 1946-dated order for 50 aircraft was modified in 1947 to call for just 48 single-seaters. Compared to earlier examples, these new machines included a reinforced and larger vertical tail to improve lateral stability and an improved fuel system. The rear fuselage was also re-contoured to smooth the air flow from the engine exhausts.

By the end of 1947 a staggering 243 MiG-9 single-seaters had been produced and plans called for a further 250 fighters and 60 trainers to be constructed in 1948. However, with the aforementioned cancellation of the UTI programme, production switched to purely single-seaters, and 302 airframes were produced in 1948. It soon became obvious that the new MiG-15, which flew in late 1947, offered far better performance and development potential so production of the *Fargo* was eventually abandoned – by which point 598 airframes had been built.

> "A small bubble canopy was fitted in the back for a flight engineer"

Nonetheless, the existing MiG-9s remained in service and were also subjected to further modifications. Two aircraft were used as development machines to try to solve the engine flame-out issues. These were fitted with a rectangular vane on the barrel of the N-37 cannon that dispersed the airflow from the weapon and allowed all three guns to be fired simultaneously. However, the vane affected the aircraft's directional stability and caused it to yaw after just five shots. Worse still, the vane was found to disintegrate after around 800 shots had been fired the debris being far more dangerous to the engine than the disturbed air!

ENGINE TEST-BEDS
Other MiG-9s were used as engine test-beds, including the MiG-9FL which was fitted with a single 3,300lb/thrust Lyulka TR-1 turbojet in place of the two 1,754lb/thrust RD-20s. In order to accommodate the new engine the MiG's armament was rearranged with the 23mm cannons moved to each side of the fuselage. The aircraft was intended to have a pressurised cockpit but the engine was delayed to such an extent that the MiG-15 beat it into the sky and the programme was cancelled.

Undeterred, MiG OKB began working on a version of the MiG-9 fitted with afterburning versions of the RD-20 powerplant. These engines had a maximum power of 2,300lb/thrust each and it was hoped these would increase the top speed of the MiG9FF variant to 513kts (590mph). The aircraft also dispensed with the N-37 gun in favour of a 1.8in (45mm) cannon and benefited from 12mm armour plating around the cockpit and a bulletproof windscreen. The first conversion flew in June 1947 but crashed during State acceptance trials in August. A second prototype was built and during trials in December it reached 511kts (588mph). However, no further development work was done and the project was cancelled.

Another unusual sub-variant of the aircraft was the MiG-9L, a 1949 conversion of a single example to test avionics for the KS-1 Kometa air-launched anti-shipping cruise missile. The MiG's armament was removed and a radome was fitted in the nose for a radar transmitter. A small pod with a radar receiver was also fitted to the leading inboard edge of each wing and a blister was fitted to the top of the tailfin to house the missile's radio control system. Finally, a second cockpit with a small bubble canopy was fitted in the middle of the aircraft's back for a flight engineer.

OPERATIONAL FLYING

Although the MiG-9 was quickly surpassed by the MiG-15 it was operated by VVS fighter regiments in the 1st, 7th, 14th, 15th, and 16th Air Armies.

In reality, the MiG-9 was a very impractical aircraft to operate. The tyres only lasted around 20 take-offs and landings and the aircraft's lack of aerodynamic drag meant it quickly wore through brakes during its long landing runs. As a result, pilots were forbidden from taxiing the aircraft under power and it was towed to and from the runway by tractor.

> **" Pilots were forbidden from taxiing the aircraft under power "**

A serious of inflight breakups and other crashes were blamed on the aircraft's handling qualities and soon after it was introduced into frontline service in 1947 the type was restricted to essentially straight and level flight.

As more became known about the idiosyncrasies of jet flight this restriction was lifted and in 1950 the aeroplane really proved its worth when six divisions (each with two regiments of 31 aircraft) were transferred to China to defend its cities against air raids by the Nationalist Chinese and train the Chinese pilots in jet operations.

The 17th Guards Fighter Aviation Division (GIAD) defended Shenyang, the 20th Fighter Aviation Division (IAD) guarded Tangshan, and the 65th IAD protected Guangzhou. The 144th IAD defended Shanghai, the 309th guarded Gongzhuling and the 328th IAD protected Peking.

Eventually the units handed their aircraft over to the People's Liberation Army Air Force when their training was complete.

Some thought was given to sending PLAAF MiG-9s to Korea in 1951 but Chinese commanders opted to retrain its pilots on MiG-15s instead.

Although the MiG-9 was in production for a short period, and saw limited operational flying, it retains an important part in Russian aviation history. It was the nation's first jet and set the MiG OKB on the path that would create some of the world's most iconic fighters. ❖

Three of the four remaining MiG-9s can be found in China, with two on public display.

Swept Wing MiGs
MiG-15 and MiG-17 – Soviet Icons

The MiG-15 was built under licence in Poland by the WSK-Mielec company. The original MiG-15 was known as the Lim-1, the MiG-15bis became the Lim-2 and the two-seat MiG-15UTU was built as the SBLim-2. One of the Polish Air Force's last examples is seen here during 1991. *KEY – Duncan Cubitt*

The incomparable MiG-15 was the Mikoyan design bureau's breakthrough jet fighter. While internationally influenced, it's nothing less than a Soviet icon – a mighty emblem of ingenuity, technical accomplishment and unrivalled longevity. Paul Fiddian looks at the making of a legend and the MiG-17 it spawned

Still in military service 70 years after first punching its way skywards, the remarkable MiG-15 is history's most produced combat jet and its outstanding success catapulted Mikoyan-Gurevich into the upper echelons of post-war aircraft design.

The MiG-15's story began with World War Two's dark shadow still in retreat. Military aviation had undergone enormous evolution during those six long years of conflict but, of all the progressions made, it was the new generation of long-range, high-flying heavy bombers that had the Soviet government particularly worried.

Thanks to Igor Sikorsky's then-monstrous four-engined Ilya Muromets, the Russian Empire had been strategic bombing's birthplace but that was back in the Great War and much global advancement had taken place since then.

Entering US Army Air Forces (USAAF) service on May 8, 1944 – exactly one year prior to Germany's surrender that ended the war in Europe – the Boeing B-29 Superfortress was an unimaginable capability leap beyond Sikorsky's famed progenitor. Being a 12-plus hour mission, August 6, 1945's atomic bombing of Hiroshima had starkly underlined that type's strategic reach and ever-increasing long-range bombing potential lay in Boeing's improved B-50 and mighty B-36 Peacemaker.

On March 21, 1946, the USAAF's Strategic Air Command (SAC) was officially inaugurated. That same month, Premier of the Soviet Union Joseph Stalin called Artem Mikoyan and several of his fighter-designing contemporaries to the Kremlin. Each was tasked with evolving, developing and test-flying an interceptor able to engage and overcome the emerging nuclear threat. The Soviet government's criteria were both rigorous and comprehensive. Mikoyan et al's creations *had* to be operationally versatile, speedy (Mach 0.9, just over 600kts or 690mph, was the target) and extensively-armed. A 36,000ft (10,973m) flight ceiling was also required, as was a one-plus hour mission endurance.

"WHAT FOOL WILL SELL US HIS SECRETS?!"

It was realised quite early on that Soviet jet engines weren't sufficiently advanced to play their part in the interceptor programme: however good the aircraft might be, the readily available powerplants couldn't match them. Great Britain then ruled the jet engine world but what prospect existed of its propulsive lead being shared with other nations? That much, Mikoyan would soon discover when he accompanied leading engine authority Vladimir Klimov and production technologist Sergey Kishkin on an explorative mission to England. The three men were shown Rolls-Royce's state-of-the-art Nene and Derwent products. The trio suitably impressed, procurement negotiations got underway. "What fool will sell us his secrets?!" Stalin had earlier asked. The response came in the Labour government's willingness to export both the technology and its supporting documentation. The UK Ministry of Defence – initially extremely reluctant to

The prototype MiG I-310 first flew on December 30, 1947 with test pilot Captain Viktor Yuganov at the controls

Of all-metal construction, MiG's final design featured sharply-swept wings derived from German research into transonic speed. Two fences, to boost aerodynamic performance, sat on each wing while an ovular, relatively stubby fuselage culminated in airbrakes and a prominent tail with a leading edge set at 56 degrees. Dimensionally, the aircraft measured 33ft 2in in length and 33ft 1in in span; figures maintained throughout the MiG-15's development.

Artem Mikoyan visited England in 1946 along with leading engine authority Vladimir Klimov and production technologist Sergey Kishkin. The three men were shown Rolls-Royce's state-of-the-art Nene and Derwent products and were suitably impressed. The willingness of Britain's Labour government to export both the technology and its supporting documentation amazed the Russians but a deal was agreed to provide ten Nenes. Reverse-engineering efforts were launched almost the instant the first consignment arrived on Soviet soil.

▲ Among Lavochkin's entries into the competition was the La-174. It was initially affected by structural vibrations but a refined successor, the La-174D resurrected the programme in late summer 1948. Unlike the MiG the aircraft's wing was placed high and its main undercarriage legs were fuselage-mounted rather than retracting into the wing. It would later evolve into the La-15 fighter, of which 235 would be built.

◄ Other types vying with the I-310 to meet the Soviet Air Forces' and Air Defence Forces' new interceptor requirement included the Yakovlev Yak-30. It first flew on September 4, 1948 but could not compete with the MiG in terms of performance.

seal the deal – agreed an introductory ten-Nenes sale in September 1946 and a follow-up order, for 15 more, six months later, with 30 Derwents supplementing these 25 Nenes.

REVERSE ENGINEERED

Reverse-engineering efforts were launched almost the instant the first consignment arrived on Soviet soil and, rapidly, indigenous copies emerged. These were designated the RD-45 (Nene 2) and RD-500 (Derwent 5) – 'RD' for reaktivniy dvigatel (jet engine) and '45'/'500' signifying the factories inside which they were built. Both were being manufactured in significant quantities within months.

Mikoyan's interceptor design was quite advanced at this stage, but the new engine's availability necessitated extensive fuselage revision. Several options surfaced and were tweaked before the classic MiG-15 profile began to take form. Of all-metal construction, the bureau's final design featured sharply-swept wings. Raked back 35 degrees, with two degrees of anhedral, these were the aircraft's gateway into the high transonic speed range required. This aspect owed much to late-war German research, with relating documents having entered Soviet possession some months before. Two fences, to boost aerodynamic performance, sat on each wing while an oval, relatively stubby fuselage culminated in airbrakes and a prominent tail with a leading edge set at 56 degrees. Dimensionally, the aircraft measured 33ft 2in (10.1 metres) in length and 33ft 1in (10.09 metres) in span; figures maintained throughout the MiG-15's development.

Among this prototype's other innovations were fire warning and extinguishing systems and a winch and steel rope-raised/lowered weapons maintenance platform. This was positioned on the nose's underside, a location that studies had established, armament-wise, produced the optimum blend of accuracy, accessibility and centre of gravity maintenance. The weapons themselves comprised a pair of Nudelman-Suranov NS-23 autocannons, fitted to port, and a single starboard-mounted Nudelman N-37 cannon. Named for their millimetric internal diameter, these weapons had an 80-round and 40-round capacity, respectively. Pilots later found that these supplied less than nine seconds' combined firing time but what they lacked in endurance, they made up for in intensity.

A bifurcated intake system fed air through to the engine that servicers and maintainers reached via hinges that swung out the rear fuselage at a point just aft of the main fuel tank. The provision to carry wing-mounted external fuel tanks, each of 55 Imp Gal (250lit) capacity, supplemented the internal 273 Imp Gal (1,240lit) supply. Pilot comfort was a primary consideration and, to that end, the aircraft had a pressurised and air-conditioned cockpit, while the bubble canopy and ejection seat – another Soviet fighter first – added elements of practicality and safety. ➡

The two-seat MiG-15UTI was designed in the space of just a month meaning a minimum amount of modifications possible were made, the two focus areas being the cockpit and fuel system. The cockpit area was extended rearwards, enabling the installation of a second ejector seat and duplicate controls, while fuel capacity was reduced and the armament quota downgraded. Here an Albanian Air Force MiG-15UTI heads out on a training sortie.

I-310 TRAILBLAZER

The Mikoyan Design Bureau named its technological trailblazer the I-310 and, by the end of 1947, it was ready to fly. Taxiing trials, at various speeds, were performed for several days while waiting for suitable weather conditions. Finally, on December 30, the I-310 got airborne and test pilot Captain Viktor Yuganov fed back a generally positive account of the prototype's first flight. Subsequent testing continued through the first quarter of 1948. Trials were still incomplete by mid-March but that didn't stop the Soviet Government fervently initiating series production, by decree number 790-255, on March 15. This early production approval would later prove a sage move.

Three I-130s were manufactured in all, with those designated S-02 and S-03 following the first airframe's (S-01) lead. As engine testbeds, they were upgraded to receive Klimov's RD-45 developments: the VK-1 and its afterburning brother, the VK-1F. They also had numerous other revisions woven into the mix. S-02 was both physically altered (revised canopy, altered wings) and, with its new S-13 gun camera and ASP-1N sighting unit, systemically enhanced, while S-03 was given airbrakes, a modified tail, surfaced-increased ailerons and enlarged fuel tanks.

S-01's final flight, on May 25, 1948, preceded S-02's maiden flight by just two days and S-03's, on July 17, by a little under two months. Phased flight-testing, at Chkalovsk, lasted much of the year's remainder – S-03 attaining, at one point, Mach 0.934 (622kts/716mph) – while a second decree, 3210-1303, signalled the start of full production on August 23. The first production example, again piloted by Yuganov, lifted off on December 30: exactly 12 months after the prototype's maiden sortie.

COMPETITORS

Other types had been vying with the I-310 to meet the Soviet Air Forces' and Air Defence Forces' new interceptor requirement. One, the Yakovlev Yak-30, was already lagging behind its rivals when first flown on September 4, 1948. RD-500-powered, it had a maximum speed of 554kts (637mph) and a ceiling of 49,213ft (15,000m). Not being of the same standard, it made little further progress beyond the starting blocks.

Lavochkin's entries were more serious competitors. The La-168 had first flown on April 22, 1948 and shared the MiG-15's powerplant and armament but not its fortune. Around ten months into testing, a cannon-induced mechanical failure proved its downfall. The prototype of its other submission, known as the La-174, was also affected by structural vibrations but a refined successor, the La-174D resurrected the programme in late summer 1948.

Mikoyan-Gurevich and Lavochkin's prototypes had much in common albeit the La-174D's wing, swept to 37.3 degrees, was placed high and its main undercarriage legs were fuselage-mounted rather than retracting into the wing.

Performance-wise, it boasted superior manoeuvrability and stability but the 1-310 had rate-of-climb, range, firepower and ease of assembly all on its side. Around 100 comparison flights produced no clear winner. Testing was thus expanded out into the operational domain using production versions of both types, now officially the MiG-15 and the La-15. Financially advantageous and a more straightforward build, the MiG-15 edged ahead and when combined frontline support provision became unsustainable, there was no catching it: Mikoyan-Gurevich's design had won. Even so, after a limited production run, the La-15 remained in service until 1954. The MiG-15, in contrast, stayed in Soviet Air Force use for at least a decade gaining the rather unflattering NATO reporting name *Fagot*.

UPGRADED 'BIS'

MiG-15 manufacture took place at a blistering pace but the initial results were far from perfect. As issues were detected, so corresponding rectifications were

The definitive single-seat version was the MiG-15bis, a number of which are seen here preparing to get airborne on an exercise.

An Algerian Air Force MiG-15bis visiting Aden in 1968. *Adrian M Balch Collection*

fed into the factory lines. This produced a miscellany of variously-configured airframes but as these early examples were being delivered, more universal series improvements were already in the works. At first given the designation MiG-15SD, this upgraded version became, as the MiG-15bis ('second'), the dominant production model. One important change saw the VK-1 permanently displace the RD-45, the earlier engine's operational weaknesses now having been exposed (in need of frequent overhauls, the RD-45 was also unreliable, didn't always produce the anticipated thrust and was fuel-thirsty).

Fitted in mid-late stage MiG-15bis models, the 5,957lb/thrust VK-1 helped to produce a machine that could hit 581kts (669mph) and climb at 8,880ft/min (2,700m/min): increases of 15kts (17mph) and 600ft/min (183m/min), respectively over the first MiG-15s. The aircraft's ceiling was raised from 49,869ft (15,200m) to 50,853ft (15,500m) and range extended from 1,217 miles (1,960km) to 1,243 miles (2,000km). Together with these performance boosts came the need for longer landing runs and, consequentially, the introduction of a braking parachute.

Among the MiG-15bis' other alterations were reshaped airbrakes, angled at 22 degrees. The cockpit was upgraded and the NS-23 guns exchanged for NR-23s that had a faster firing rate. Later, two 255lb (116kg) ARS-212 or four 101lb (46kg) TRS-190 rockets boosted the weapons complement. Customers for the enhanced MiG-15 included China; deliveries to the People's Liberation Army Air Force (PLAAF) first took place in 1950 and the aircraft's use would continue into the late 1980s.

TWO-SEAT UTI

Next from the Mikoyan Design Bureau came a two-seat trainer version: the MiG-15 UTI (Uchebno-Trenirovochnyy Istrebitel). Work on this began at Factory 1 in the spring of 1949 and was necessarily fast-paced – Mikoyan-Gurevich's design team having been given only around one month's development time!

The tight scheduling naturally limited the number of modifications possible; the two focus areas being the cockpit and fuel system. The cockpit area was extended rearwards, enabling the installation of a second ejector seat and duplicate controls, while fuel capacity was reduced and the armament quota downgraded. Carrying the designation I-312T, the UTI prototype took flight on May 23, 1949. The engine used was the 5,005lb/thrust RD-45F and this powered the two-place MiG to a maximum of 548kts (631mph). Peak flight level was 47,982ft (14,625m) and the top end of its range was 870 miles (1,400km).

Both the MiG-15bis and MiG-15UTI entered mass production in 1950. This was the most intensive production year yet, with 1,911 single-seat and 56 two-seat '15s' rolling off the factory lines (the MiG Design Bureau built the prototypes but remote factories, some located hundreds of miles away, undertook series production).

There were eight other factories, besides No 1, within which MiG-15s were pieced together. These were numbered 153 (Novosibirsk), 381 (Leningrad), 21 (Gorky), 31 (Tbilisi), 126 (Komsomo'ls'k-na-Amure) 292 (Saratov), 135 (Kharkiv) and 99 (Ulan-Ude). Manufacturing hit an all-time high in 1951, when an incredible 4,033 fighter models and 450 trainers were produced. 1952's 3,020 MiG-15bis total occurred in that model's last major production year but MiG-15UTI assembly was yet to reach its zenith. It did so in 1954 (1,133 examples completed) and continued, although at much more conservative levels, until 1959. By this point, the nine factories were responsible, between them, for some 11,000 MiG-15s.

Reflecting only activity within the USSR, these figures are astonishing enough but don't factor in the Czech or Polish licence-build programmes that contributed around 5,000 examples to the total of circa 16,000 MiG-15s manufactured worldwide.

Several MiG-15 display teams were formed, most notably the Soviet Air Force's *Red Five* group which flew a five-ship in a striking two-tone scarlet and aluminium scheme.

Czech firm Avia produced licence built versions of the MiG-15 (S-102), MiG-15bis (S-103) and MiG-15UTI (CS-102). The first examples entered service from mid-1951 onwards.

Hungary was another former Eastern Bloc nation to be armed with the prolific MiG-15.

A gun camera photo of a MiG-15 being attacked by a USAF F-86A Sabre during the Korean War. *USAF Museum*

Czech firm Avia's activity resulted in the S-102 (MiG-15), S-103 (MiG-15bis) and CS-102 (MiG-15UTI). Their Polish equivalents, that WSK-Mielec created, were the Lim-1, Lim-2 and SBLim-2. Both the Czechoslovak and Polish air forces placed their locally-built examples in service from mid-1951 onwards.

Conceived as a mere conversion platform, the MiG-15UTI became the Eastern Bloc's standard jet trainer. The absence of MiG-17 and MiG-19 training versions gave it a prolonged service life and thrust it into some 36 nations' inventories.

While the MiG-15, MiG-15bis and MiG-15UTI were the main models, a raft of more specialised variants also joined the series, such as the bis-based MiG-15P. This was a radar-equipped nightfighter that was put into limited production. The MiG-15-bisR was a dedicated reconnaissance model, fitted with a neck-mounted camera, while the -bisS was, with its increased fuel capacity, intended for bomber escort duties. One further MiG-15bis modification saw an air-to-air refuelling system added. Two aircraft were converted and the experiment got so far as airborne trials involving a Tupolev Tu-4 *Bull*: the Soviet Air Force's reverse-engineered B-29. These didn't go well however and vapour ingress into the MiG's cockpit was just one of the many issues that preceded the concept's abandonment.

TO WAR IN KOREA

On June 25, 1950, North Korea attacked South Korea. It was an unapologetically violent application of force that ignited three years of conflict, into which a host of other countries were drawn. Airpower was a prominent part of the Korean War, especially early-on.

Sequential United Nations (UN) Security Council resolutions – 82-to-85, adopted between June 25 and July 31 – rapidly brought member states' military assets to the region in support of South Korea. Operating within the structure of UN Command, USAF F-80 Shooting Stars and F-84 Thunderjets, US Navy F9F Panthers and numerous other Western types met with North Korean People's Army Air Force fighters in increasingly-turbulent skies.

The latter's La-9s and Yak-9s could put up little resistance and became swiftly overwhelmed. Similarly, the USAF's B-29s bombing missions, that wreaked devastation on North Korean terrain, proceeded virtually unchallenged. Then, in swept the wind of change, MiG-15s astride its crest, and back swung the see-saw of success.

MiG-15 combat sorties didn't begin over Korea – the type's first shoot-down had in fact been achieved some months earlier, during the Chinese Civil War – but it was there that the aircraft's ruthless reputation was established and solidified.

That initial engagement was against a Taiwanese Lockheed P-38 Lightning – but now the MiG started to face increasingly more potent adversaries.

Its overall first, and first jet fighter 'kills' of the Korean War, happened within hours of each other on November 1, 1950. That day's F-51 Mustang and F-80 Shooting Star downings were each the work of a Soviet Air Force example equipping its 50th IAD (Istrebitelnaya Aviadiviziya – Fighter Aviation Division).

Bombers, too, were heavily targeted, the MiG-15 here performing the interceptor role for which it had been designed. One especially effective interception tactic saw flights of MiG-15s swarm at high-altitude before bombarding the UN force aircraft from above. Now portioned up into smaller groups, they would launch an omnidirectional attack of the type that, on April 12, 1951, unleashed havoc upon a large mixed USAF types formation that included no less than 48 B-29s. A total of 44 MiG-15s had been loitering in wait and they ended up damaging or destroying ten of the transiting Superfortresses, plus a trio of F-80s and one other type, for the loss of just one of their own.

Word of this ferocious new Soviet fighter soon began to spread. The Western world, it's fair to say, was somewhat rattled. "Not only is it faster than anything we are building today, but it is already being produced in very large numbers", proclaimed then-Marshall of the Royal Air Force, Sir John Slessor. "The Russians, therefore, have achieved a four-year lead over British development in respect of the

Left: The Royal Ceylon Air Force first went into combat in 1971 when the Marxist JVP launched an island-wide insurrection on April 5. During this insurgency the left-leaning Bandaranaike government turned to the Soviet Union for more sophisticated weaponry to replace its BAC Jet Provosts, and received five Mikoyan-Gurevich MiG-17F fighter-bombers and a MiG-15 UTI trainer. **Right:** In 1955, Egypt made an agreement to buy heavy arms from Czechoslovakia in an attempt to move away from reliance on British armaments. Initial Soviet bloc deliveries included up to 100 MiG-15s, Ilyushin Il-28 bombers, Ilyushin Il-14 transports, and Yak-11 trainers.

SPECIFICATION MIKOYAN-GUREVICH MIG-15BIS

Key Publishing – Pete West

Crew	1	**Service Ceiling**	50,840ft (15,500m)
Length	33ft 2in (10.10m)	**Combat Range**	1,565 miles (2,520km)
Wingspan	33ft 1in (10.09m)	**Powerplant**	One 5,950lb/thrust Klimov VK-1 centrifugal-flow turbojet
Height	12ft 2in (3.70m)		
Wing Area	222ft² (20.5m²)	**Armament**	
Empty Weight	8,113lbs (3,681kg)	Two 23mm Nudelman-Rikhter NR-23 autocannons in the lower left fuselage, one 37mm Nudelman N-37 autocannon in the lower right fuselage and two hardpoints for 220lb (100kg) bombs or unguided rockets	
Loaded Weight	11,177lbs (5,044kg)		
Max Speed	(Sea level) 581kts (669mph/1,076km/h)		
Max Speed	(at 10,000ft) 599kts (688mph/1,107km/h)		

vitally important interceptor fighter". It did so, remember, with the benefit of British engine technology.

MIG ALLEY

Not to be irreversibly disadvantaged, the West reacted quickly: come mid-December, USAF North American F-86A Sabres had arrived in theatre. Starting on December 17, 1950, many months of era-defining air-to-air encounters would follow, with one particularly frenetic combat area, above North Korea's Yalu River/Yellow Sea join, becoming known as 'MiG Alley'.

The MiG-15 and F-86A were on a generally even keel but each boasted particular advantages. The MiG had greater vertical reach (50,853ft vs 45,000ft) and a better rate of climb but the Sabre was the superior diver and was more agile to boot. Fitted with six 12.7mm M3 Browning machine guns, each able to fire 300 rounds, the Sabre boasted inherently greater firepower but the MiG's NR-23s and N-37 combination packed a greater punch.

These machines' capabilities so closely aligned, it was pilot experience that tended to seal each encounter's fate. Better training had produced a cadre of USAF pilots that swiftly managed to unlock the local airspace from the MiG's snarling grip: 123 MiG-15s falling to the earth during one three-month stretch. Their Chinese and North Korean equivalents just couldn't maintain parity but it was a different story with a well-trained Russian pilot – as happened many times – in the hot-seat. Ultimately, USAF F-86s claimed 792 MiG-15s for 78 losses: a 10-to-one advantage, although that's according to contemporary US military combat records whose accuracy has since been questioned. The conflict's top Russian MiG-15 ace was Captain Nikolai Sutyagin. His 21 kills included nine F-86s, an F-84 and a Meteor. For this, he received the Hero of the Soviet Union decoration, as did 19 other participating Soviet pilots.

There were many other Cold War-era MiG-15 actions of note, not least of which was the type's participation in the Suez and Taiwan Straits crises. One of the more unusual – the so-called Catalina Affair – began on June 13, 1952. It saw a Soviet Air Force MiG-15s pair shoot down a Swedish Air Force Tp 79 (C-47 Skytrain) that was on a covert intelligence-gathering mission over the Baltic Sea. All on board perished. A Tp 47 (Catalina) from the same air arm was dispatched on search and rescue duties three days later but it, too, was lost to MiG-fire, this time without fatal consequences.

Mention must also be made of the several MiG-15 display teams formed during this period, although little is now known of them beyond their existence. Within its *Red Five* series that stretched across many fighters' lifespans, the Soviet Air Force fielded a five-ship team in a striking two-tone scarlet and aluminium scheme. The Czechoslovak Air Force, too, formed a formation unit of similarly-coloured S-102s that were active for much of the 1950s.

MIG-17 FRESCO

While the MiG-15 *Fagot* was wreaking havoc in the skies over Korea, the Mikoyan-Gurevich Design Bureau had been working on its replacement since 1949.

Originally dubbed the MiG-15bis45, the new type was created to both remedy problems found within the basic fighter design and operate at a much higher Mach number.

Although the resulting MiG-17 – which was dubbed *Fresco* by NATO – strongly resembled its forebear, it had an entirely new thinner and more highly swept wing and tailplane. The wing itself was swept at a 45-degree angle near the fuselage and a 42-degree angle further outboard. Although it was thinner, the wing was stiffer than that of the earlier aircraft to resist the tendency to 'flex' at its wingtips and therefore lose aerodynamic symmetry unexpectedly at high speeds or wing loads.

Other readily visible differences to its predecessor were the addition of a third wing fence on each wing, and a ventral fin and a longer and less tapered rear fuselage that resulted in the aircraft growing from 33ft 2in (10.10m) to 37ft (11.26m) in length.

Early MiG-17s shared the same Klimov VK-1 engine, forward fuselage undercarriage and armament as the MiG-15, all of which helped the prototype I-330 to fly as early as January 14, 1950. Test pilot Ivan Ivashchenko was at the helm.

Just three months later on March 17, Ivashchenko was killed when his aircraft developed flutter that tore off its horizontal tail mid-flight. Lack of wing stiffness also resulted in aileron reversal which was discovered and fixed by the time the SI-2 prototype flew in early 1951. The MiG-17 was accepted for production on September 1, 1951. Construction and

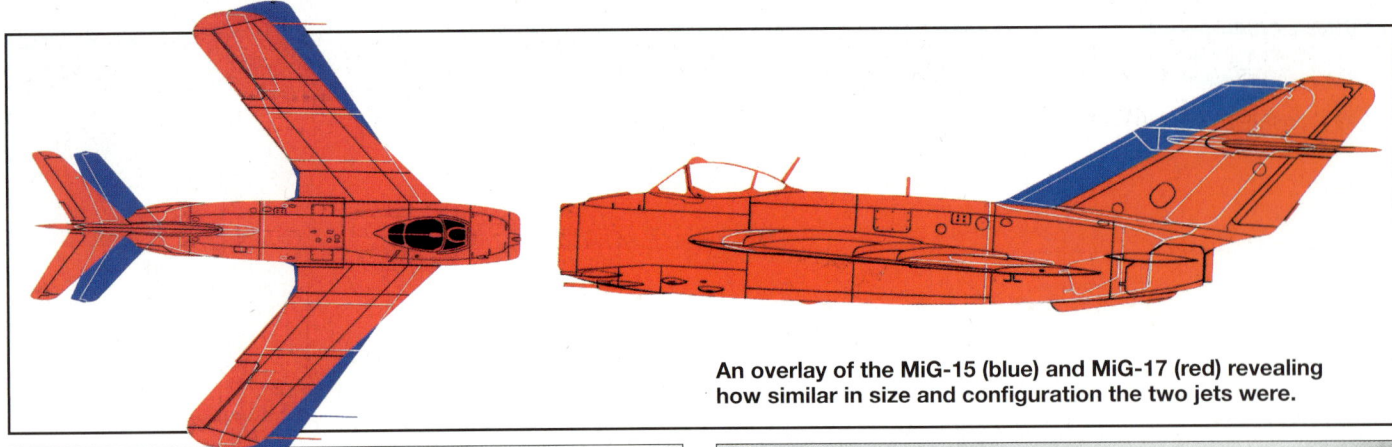

An overlay of the MiG-15 (blue) and MiG-17 (red) revealing how similar in size and configuration the two jets were.

A quartet of Red Air Force MiG-17s on patrol in the mid-1950s.

North Vietnamese Air Force pilots smile for the camera alongside their newly delivered MiG-17s in 1964.

Left: PZL-Mielec produced the MiG-17 under licence in Poland as the Lim-5 and Lim-6. **Right:** An Egyptian MiG-17 overflies the forward command post of the IDF's 162nd Armoured Division during the October War in 1973. *USAF Museum*

tests of additional SI-2 prototypes and experimental series aircraft SI-02 and SI-01 in 1951, were generally successful.

On September 1, 1951, the aircraft was accepted for production and even the early non-reheated examples benefited from a 27kts (31mph) increase in speed compared to the MiG-15 (despite using the same powerplant). The new fighter also demonstrated greater manoeuvrability at high-altitude.

Priority was given to getting MiG-15s into the hands of squadron pilots in large numbers so although the MiG-17 was underway by the third quarter of 1951 it did not enter service until October 1952 – by which time the MiG-19 was almost ready for flight testing.

The MiG-17 was optimised as a general-purpose day fighter and as such was armed with one Nudelman N-37 37mm cannon and two 23mm cannons. It could also act as a fighter-bomber but usually carried additional fuel tanks instead of ordnance.

The optical gunsight and SRD-3 gun ranging radar from a captured F-86 Sabre were copied to produce the MiG-17's ASP-4N gunsight and SRC-3 radar and from 1953, pilots also got safer ejection seats with a protective face curtain and leg restraints.

Updated versions of the new fighter included the radar equipped *Fresco A* and the all-weather-capable MiG-17P (*Fresco B*) but the most important development came with the 1953 introduction of the MiG-17F (*Fresco C*). The 'F' indicated the presence of the afterburning VK-1F engine and a new convergent-divergent nozzle and fuel system. The afterburner doubled the rate of climb and while the MiG-17 was not designed to be supersonic, skilled pilots could push it through the sound barrier in a shallow dive – although the fighter would often pitch up just short of Mach 1.

The MiG-17F would be the most popular variant of the breed but the next mass-produced version, the MiG-17PF *Fresco D* incorporated a more powerful Izumrud RP-2 radar. In 1956 a series of 47 aircraft were converted to MiG-17PM standard to enable them to carry four first-generation Kaliningrad K-5 air-to-air missiles.

A small series of MiG-17R reconnaissance aircraft were also built with the VK-1F engine and by the time production ended in the USSR in 1958, almost 8,000 examples had been built. More than 3,000 other airframes were constructed under licence in Poland as the

SPECIFICATION MIKOYAN-GUREVICH MIG-17F

Key Publishing – Pete West

Length	37ft 0in (11.26m)	Combat Range	1,255 miles (2,020km)
Wingspan	31ft 7in (9.63m)	Powerplant:	One 7,423lb/thrust Klimov VK-1F
Height	12ft 6in (3.80m)		afterburning centrifugal-flow turbojet
Wing Area	243ft² (22.6m²)	Armament	
Empty Weight	8,640lbs (3,919kg)	Two 23mm Nudelman-Rikhter NR-23 autocannons	
Loaded Weight	13,375lbs (5,340kg)	in the lower left fuselage, one 37mm Nudelman N-37	
Max Speed	(Sea level) 594kts (684mph/1,100km/h)	autocannon in the lower right fuselage and two	
Max Speed	(at 10,000ft) 619kts (712mph/1,145km/h)	hardpoints for 1,100lb (500kg) of bombs or	
Service Ceiling	54,450ft (16,600m)	unguided rockets	

WSK-Mielec Lim-5), Czechoslovakia and China – the latter producing the MiG-17F as the Shenyang J-5 (for domestic use) or F-5 (for export). Elsewhere in the world the MiG-17 would fly with the air arms of 20 nations.

VIETNAM COMBAT

Although the MiG-17 was not flown operationally during the Korean War, the type was to see its first combat over the Straits of Taiwan when Communist People's Republic of China MiG-17s clashed with the Republic of China-(Nationalist China) operated F-86 Sabres in 1958. The *Fresco* had been designed to intercept straight-and-level-flying enemy bombers, not dogfighting with other fighters but they acquitted themselves well in the air-to-air combat role.

In 1960, the first group of North Vietnamese Air Force (NVAF) airmen were transferred to China to begin training onto the MiG-17. By 1962 the first pilots had graduated and the USSR sent 36 MiG-17 fighters and MiG-15UTI trainers to Hanoi

This MiG-17 was shot down by an F-105D on June 3, 1967. *USAF Museum*

in February 1964 as a 'gift'. Initially, these were the only types available to oppose modern American supersonic jets before MiG-19s and MiG-21s were introduced into North Vietnamese service from 1969.

Despite being outdated and much slower than their opponents, three of the 16 NVAF aces of the war were MiG-17 pilots – the aircraft's manoeuvrability making up for what it lacked in speed.

By 1972, NVAF MiG-17s had claimed 71 aerial victories against US aircraft: 11 Vought F-8 Crusaders, 16 Republic F-105 Thunderchiefs, 32 McDonnell Douglas F-4 Phantom IIs, two Douglas A-4 Skyhawks, seven Douglas A-1 Skyraiders, one C-47 cargo/transport aircraft, one Sikorsky CH-3C helicopter and one Ryan Firebee UAV.

In 2018 a handful of MiG-15 and 17s remain airworthy around the globe. Today, the Korean People's Army Air Force is the only military operator of the MiG-15 – with four UTI variants still in service. Elsewhere, a wealth of MiG-15s are airworthy in private ownership.

When it comes to the MiG-17, examples are still on strength with the air forces of the Democratic Republic of the Congo, Guinea, Mali, Madagascar, Sudan, and Tanzania. Chinese J-5 variants also fly in China and North Korea.

The Mikoyan Design Bureau would create faster-flying, further-reaching types but all owed their success to the unparalleled MiG-15. ❖

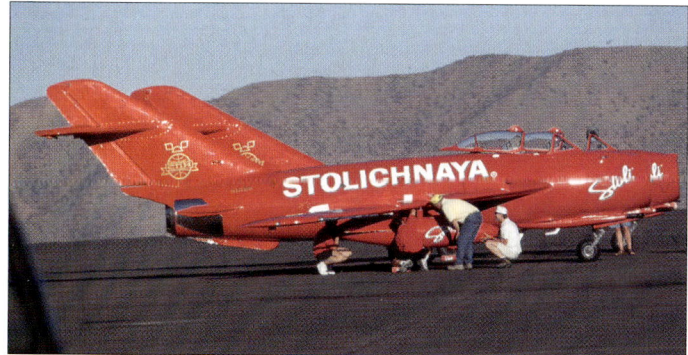

Left: This pair of privately owned MiG-17s were operated on the USA circuit for many years and sponsored by Stoli vodka. They are seen here at the National Championship Air Races at Reno, Nevada in the late 1990s. **Right:** The MiG-17F Fresco C introduced the afterburner to the family for the first time. The aircraft was fitted with a reheat enabled VK-1F engine and a new convergent-divergent nozzle and fuel system. The afterburner doubled the rate of climb, as demonstrated by this privately-owned example at the 2014 EAA AirVenture show at Oshkosh, Wisconsin. *Steve Bridgewater*

The Victorious Underdog

On August 9, 1952, at the height of the Korean War, Commander Peter 'Hoagy' Carmichael achieved notoriety by shooting down a MiG-15 jet with a piston-powered Sea Fury. Kimberley Hawkins looks at the controversial kill.

As Commander Peter 'Hoagy' Carmichael led his flight of four Hawker Sea Fury FB.11s between Chinnampo and Pyongyang on August 9, 1952 the Korean War was already in full swing. The North Korean forces were fast getting to grips with their MiG-15 jets and combat with USAF F-86 Sabres was commonplace.

On this day 'Hoagy' (who took his nickname from the famous American singer and bandleader Hoagy Carmichael) and his wingmen had launched from HMS *Ocean* on a 'routine' sortie to attack the railway facilities at Manchon. The mission was to prove anything but 'routine.'

VETERAN

'Hoagy' Carmichael was already a combat veteran, having seen action during the later days of World War Two. Born on August 11, 1923 he had attended Worksop College where he was a renowned rugby player; playing for both the Rest of England versus Home Counties and the North of England Public Schools in 1941.

He joined the Royal Navy in 1942 and after pilot training in the US and South Africa was selected to fly both the Supermarine Seafire and the large Vought F4U Corsair before the war's end.

He would later convert onto the Blackburn Firebrand before joining 802 Naval Air Squadron's (NAS) Sea Fury fleet in June 1948.

KOREA

In November 1951 Carmichael, along with the rest of 802 NAS, received notification that the squadron would deploy to Korea in early 1952. The deployment began with a short voyage to Malta aboard HMS *Theseus* and was followed by an intensive work-up period at RNAS Hal Far.

The squadron embarked on HMS *Ocean* in April and sailed for Korea, stopping off in Hong Kong to pick up additional aircraft and pilots.

SEA FURY

802 NAS was equipped with the Hawker Sea Fury FB.11 in Korea, a type that would become the Royal Navy's last piston powered fighter aircraft and, in due course, the fastest British piston-powered aircraft of all time. An evolutionary ancestor to the Hawker Typhoon and Tempest, the Sea Fury was powered by a 2,480hp Bristol Centaurus 18-cylinder radial engine. This gave it a maximum speed of 400kts (460mph) which, combined with an impressive turning performance, made it one of the most capable piston fighters ever built.

ENGAGEMENT

On August 9, 1952 'Hoagy' was flying Sea Fury WJ232, his regular squadron mount and was accompanied by his usual 'Number 2' Sub-Lieutenant Carl Haines as well as Lieutenant Pete Davies (Number 3) and Lieutenant Brian 'Schmoo' Ellis (Number 4).

On this particular day, there were no Sabres providing top cover for the ground attack fighters and as Manchon was close to the mouth of the Yalu River, the notorious MiG Alley was a short transit from where the Sea Furies were operating.

The group had been in the area for around 20 minutes, flying at 4,000ft (1,219m) and searching for trains to attack, when Sub-Lieutenant Haines became the first to spot the enemy and gave a radio warning that eight MiGs were about to attack.

At first 'Hoagy' couldn't get visual with the North Korean jets but 'Schmoo' Ellis called for the squadron to break formation when he noticed tracer streaming past his cockpit. The fight was on.

All four pilots jettisoned their drop tanks immediately. 'Schmoo', however, found that one of his would not detach and fought the rest of the engagement with about 30 Imp Gal (136lit) of fuel on one side.

Hoagy Carmichael later said: "It soon became apparent that four MiGs were after each section of two Furies, but by continuing our break turns, we presented impossible targets."

The MiGs were at least 175kts (200mph) faster than the Sea Fury, but what the piston aircraft lacked in speed it made up for in firepower. The British fighter's four 20mm cannon were ideally suited for close combat and with experienced crew, such as 'Hoagy', the Sea Fury was a powerful fighting machine.

MiG DOWN

As the formation of Navy fighters split into pairs in a 'scissors' manoeuvre, the MiGs made their attack, streaking fast into the formation. The usual MiG pilot tactic was to 'hit and run', using the jet's superior speed to get away to safety.

But, on this occasion, it appears that one of the MiG pilots chose a different tack – opting to pop open his airbrakes and take on the Sea Furies in a turning dogfight. This was to prove a fatal mistake.

'Hoagy's' own description of the action, as quoted in his obituary in the *Daily Telegraph* states: "Suddenly a MiG came down behind me: I turned towards him and, as he flew past me, I noticed he had his air brakes out. He made the mistake of trying to dogfight with us. I put my gyro sight on him and started to fire. At this point he realised he was in trouble and put his dive brakes in and started to accelerate like mad. I held him quite easily and my bullets started to hammer him. He started to roll over on his back and crashed into the ground with no attempt to bail out."

Controversy remains as to what actually happened that day. Some claim the accounts of various pilots have become melded into one and the 802 Sqn diary (written by 'Schmoo' Ellis) states that the MiG went 'head-to-head' with Lieutenant Carmichael and Sub Lieutenant Haines before turning towards Lieutenant Davies and Sub-Lieutenant Ellis. All four pilots reported seeing shells hit the MiG and two other MiGs were reported damaged during the skirmish. So it could be said that all four Sea Fury pilots acquitted themselves well.

It is doubtful that the identity of the unknown MiG pilot will ever be confirmed. However, as the combat took place in the latter stages of the war and occurred as a result of a basic tactical error, it is likely he was a newly trained Chinese or North Korean pilot with little experience.

PROPAGANDA

Just who actually downed the MiG will probably never be known, but the Royal Navy seized on a propaganda coup with 'Hoagy' Carmichael cast in the role of the plucky British underdog bloodying the nose of a faster, more modern enemy.

The Sea Fury's returned to HMS *Ocean* for a hero's reception and 'Hoagy' was sent home to be feted. He would later be awarded a Distinguished Service Cross (DSC) for his part in the fight and would go onto fly the Hawker Sea Hawk and become Officer Commanding 806 NAS at Lossiemouth. He retired from the Fleet Air Arm in 1984 and died in 1997 at the age of 73.

In hindsight it would appear that the Fleet Air Arm wanted a simple story for the media of the day and a single pilot making a single kill was what the reporters craved. 'Hoagy' Carmichael always pointed out that the credit should go to the entire flight, not just himself, but it is his name that appears in the record books.

Nevertheless, regardless of which pilot or pilots fired the fatal shot, the loss of a jet fighter to a piston powered counterpart remains a remarkable feat and one that was not repeated until the Vietnam War when a Douglas Skyraider also managed to shoot down a MiG. ❖

Peter 'Hoagy' Carmichael hauls his Sea Fury into a tight evading turn as the smoking MiG dives away. The jet would later roll onto its back and crash into the ground. Andy Hay/www.flyingart.co.uk

MiG-19
The Fighting *Farmer*

A Chinese Shenyang J-6 at the end of a training sortie.

Overshadowed by its more famous brethren, the MiG-19 was widely exported and flown by 27 nations around the world. Todd Shugart explains why the Russian *Farmer* deserves greater recognition

The MiG-19 *Farmer* was the first mass produced supersonic fighter in the world, with one of the longest service periods. Approximately 5,500 MiG-19s of all versions were produced in the USSR as well as Czechoslovakia (as the Avia S-105) and People's Republic of China (as the Shenyang J-6). The aircraft saw service with the air forces of Russia, Czechoslovakia, Cuba, North Vietnam, Egypt, Pakistan and North Korea. And yet it is one of the least recognised MiG jets in the history of Soviet aviation.

The demand for the MiG-19 came from the overarching desire to match the West in fighter jet performance. After World War Two, the Soviet Union found itself lagging behind in the advanced technologies of jet fighter development and attempted to remedy this with the MiG-15 and the MiG-17. But to counter the threat of Western long range reconnaissance aircraft that were beginning to encroach and penetrate Soviet borders with seeming impunity, Russia needed a supersonic swept-wing fighter with a faster rate of climb and higher service ceiling than any existing designs.

In April 1951 the MiG design bureau was given the order to develop its MiG-17 into a new fighter projected to attain Mach 1 (626kts/720mph) at 6,600ft (2,000m).

POWERING UP

The MiG-19 began life as Project SM-1 (I-340). The new fighter was designed around the SI-02 version of the MiG-17 prototype, whose fuselage was lengthened and widened to accommodate two Mikulin AM-5 non-after-burning jet engines side by side, which each producing around 4,400lb/thrust.

The I-340 first flew on April 19, 1952 and it was quickly surmised that the prototype suffered from poor cockpit pressurisation and the engines proved temperamental with rapid throttle movements frequently causing flameouts and surges.

The powerplants were upgraded to the 4,700lb/thrust AM-5A – which created more power than the reheated Klimov VK-1F while providing better fuel economy, but even with the larger engines the aircraft was barely supersonic so an afterburning version with AM-5F engines was produced. Additional fuel tanks were added and a braking parachute with associated tail unit housing were installed. However even with these changes it was decided to develop a new prototype and this was the SM-2 or (I-360).

The SM-2 (I-360) incorporated these changes and many more such as the installation of N-37D 37mm cannons installed with one in each wing root. The wingspan was shortened, the fuselage extended, and the overall weight increased by almost 4,000lbs (1814kg). It could also carry 200 Imp Gal (909 lit) drop tanks and featured only one wing fence on the top of each wing as opposed to three carried on the SM-1. But the most telling difference was the incorporation of a high T-tail. However, this proved troublesome and almost led to the loss of one of the SM-2 prototypes.

Flight testing began on May 24, 1952 and once again more changes were required. The engines were still not producing the thrust that was needed and it was decided to upgrade to the AM-9F. The new pair of engines added approximately 1,200lbs more thrust and the prototype was now renamed the SM-

▲ The MiG-19 was flawed from the start but eventually matured into a capable fighter.

▶ MiG-19 and MiG-15 crews line up for inspection during the 1960s.

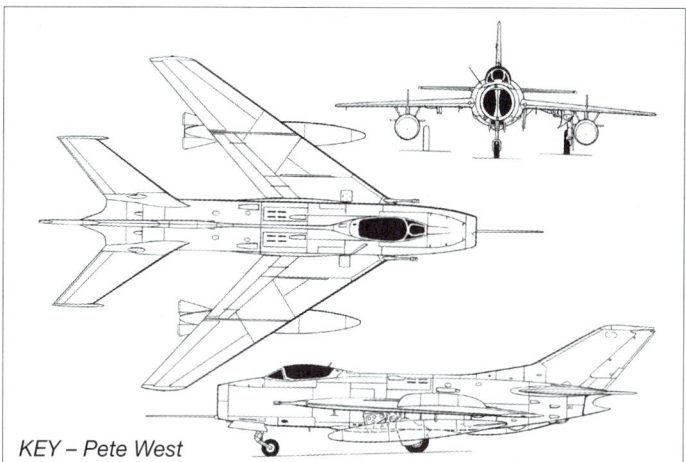
KEY – Pete West
The MiG-19 had a highly swept-wing and was the fastest of all the swept-wing MiGs that trace their histories back to the MiG-15.

A Soviet Air Force MiG-19 armed with four Kaliningrad K-5 air-to-air missiles.

9/1. A second prototype named SM-9/2 made its first flight on January 5, 1954 and was intended to be the last model before production began. However more changes followed and the armament was changed from 37mm cannons to 23mm cannons in the wing roots and a single 37mm cannon was added under the right side of the nose. This was the final version before what would later be called the MiG-19 was ordered into production.

PRODUCTION MODELS

The MiG-19 was ordered into production on February 17, 1954 even though the testing of the SM-9/1 and SM-9/2 was still ongoing! NATO gave it the reporting name *Farmer*.

The production models removed the SM-9/1 and SM-9/2's extra canopy railings for improved pilot vision and featured a tail radar warning receiver, the reintroduction of a radar range finder for the gunsight, deletion of wing pitot tubes, and a shorter nose.

The first Soviet units received the MiG-19 *Farmer-A* model in March 1955. However the first public unveiling of the MiG-19 took place on July 3, 1955 at the Air Parade over Tushino Air Base near Moscow.

The MiG-19 *Farmer-A* served with Soviet Frontal Aviation and Air Defence Regiments and unlike future variants it was never exported. However, the advantages in climb rate and service ceiling of the MiG-19 contrasted with some of the initial pilot reports and it was found to be much more demanding to fly than the MiG-15 and MiG-17. The controls were less effective at supersonic speeds and there were a high number of unexplained accidents where the aircraft would explode quite suddenly without any communications from the pilot. It turned out that putting a fuel tank near two engines that were already sat close together allowed for a significant amount of heat transferring to the aft fuel tank with the resulting explosion being quite catastrophic! The solution was to put a more robust heat shield between this fuel tank and the engines in the next variant. Sadly this problem was never truly fixed and there continued to be many related engine problems in future variants.

The MiG-19S *Farmer-C* featured a new tail section in response to pilot reports of less effective controls at supersonic speeds and when combined with the new flight control system this went a long way in improving the high speed flight performance.

Left: An early MiG-19 production aircraft awaiting test flying at the MiG factory. **Right:** The MiG-19PM *Farmer-E* variant of 1957 had the cannons removed and was armed with four Kaliningrad K-5M *Alkali* beam-riding missiles.

An Albanian Air Force MiG-19 lands back after a sortie with its drogue 'chute billowing in the breeze.

Arming Red Air Force MiG-19s on the flightline.

An East German MiG-19PM undergoing maintenance

The 23mm cannons in the wing roots were changed back to 30mm cannons and the engines were replaced with RD-9B 7,165lb/thrust engines – which increased fuel consumption. It became a standard fit for the MiG-19S *Farmer-C* to carry a pair of 200 Imp Gal (909lit) drop tanks to counter this higher fuel consumption. The accompanying decrease in max speed was also countered with longer range due to these drop tanks.

To counter the pitch down movement that occurred when the original pair of airbrakes were deployed, a third airbrake was mounted on the rear centreline of the aircraft to create a pitch up movement. These changes led to a much improved version of the MiG-19 and would also play a role in attracting interest from other countries with an eye to producing it under license.

EXPORT VALUE

By this time the MiG-19 in Soviet use was already beginning to lose favour and be replaced by more modern interceptors like the MiG-21; however, it would continue to play a key role in many other air forces.

The Bulgarian Air Force was the first country outside the Soviet Union to be equipped with the MiG-19. It took delivery of the MiG-19S in 1957 and was soon followed by Czechoslovakia and East Germany – the prior being the first of two countries allowed to build the MiG-19S under license using the designation Aero S-105. These Czech MiG-19s stayed in service until 1972. There was even a Czech Air Force display team flying MiG-19s for a period of time. Egypt was the first county outside of the Warsaw Pact to receive the MiG-19 in 1958; however, a large number of these were destroyed in the Six Day War with Israel in 1967. But by far the biggest operator of the MiG-19 was and still is the Chinese.

The Chinese began production of what would be called the Shenyang J-6 in 1958 and to this day there are still some J-6s in the People's Liberation Army Air Force (PLAAF) albeit in a new role. Over 4,500 examples of the J-6 have been produced in China alone. Chinese J-6s were very active in the 1960s and shot down at least 14 aircraft from the USAF, the USN, and the Republic of China (Taiwan). Some of these were on reconnaissance missions and some were merely off course from their targets in North Vietnam.

By far the strangest use of the J-6 is the current mission of all remaining Chinese J-6s. There are reports of a brigade of retired J-6s being converted into unmanned drones and used as decoys against an adversary's integrated air defence system. In essence they would absorb any surface-to-air missile launches or carry jammers to confuse and disrupt the opponent's air defences. This can only be considered a novel way to dispose of old airframes but in a somewhat innovative way.

One of the most notable countries to purchase and employ the F-6 (export version) was Pakistan in 1965. The Pakistanis required the F-6 to be modified and after a local modification program the F-6 was equipped with a Martin-Baker ejection seat and the ability to employ AIM-9 missiles. The Pakistan Air Force (PAF) used them to great effect against the Indian Air Force in the Third Indo-Pakistani War in December 1971. The F-6 had a long and illustrious career with the PAF and was only retired in 2002 with the Nanchang A-5 remaining even longer with their retirement in 2011. The A-5 is basically a reworked J-6/MiG-19 design and heavily modified for close air support and air interdiction. It did share some commonalities with the J-6 but after all the testing and design changes there was, in fact, not much in common!

Another notable export country was North Vietnam. The J-6/MiG-19S was brought into service at the height of the Vietnam War in 1969 but in a strange twist of fate it was delivered long after the more capable MiG-21 had already entered service. It also didn't see any significant combat until May 1972 during the *Linebacker* I USAF bombing operation over North Vietnam. The 925th Fighter Regiment was the only unit to fly the F-6, and while it was not very successful (there were no aces that flew the F-6) the highest scoring ace USAF team of Maj Bob Lodge and Capt Roger Locher were shot down by an F-6; Lodge being killed and Locher being rescued later after a long evasion

The MiG-19 served in the Bulgarian Air Force from 1958 to 1973.

A Bulgarian MiG-19 pilot climbs into his aircraft during 1967.

Left: USAF personnel inspect an Egyptian F-6 aircraft during the joint exercise *Bright Star '83*. *USAF Museum*
Right: South Korean soldiers guard a North Korean MiG-19 at their base in Suwon, south of Seoul shortly after 30-year-old North Korean pilot Lee Chui-Soo defected to the base in 1996. He received an award of more than half a million US dollars.

ordeal. Needless to say there were many other countries that flew the MiG-19 and the Chinese made F-6 - this is only a small representation of some of the more notable countries to use the type.

EXPERIMENTAL AIRCRAFT

The MiG-19 was also involved in many strange and unusual experiments such as launching from the belly of a Tu-95 *Bear* bomber and stationary launches from a towed launch vehicle that could be parked in a clearing in the woods. This latter method involved a large detachable booster rocket added to the underside of the aft fuselage. Air-to air-refuelling trials were undertaken using a Tu-16 *Badger* bomber. This was done early in the MiG-19's development period and is notable for the method it used. The hose would be released from the right wingtip of the *Badger* and it would trail back with a small drogue chute until caught by a grapple mounted in the left wingtip of the MiG-19. Once contact was secured fuel began to flow and this experiment proved

Air-to-air refuelling trials were undertaken with the Tu-16 and used a wingtip to wingtip hose system.

successful but was not adopted due to the limitation it imposed on the *Badger* fleet and the single point refuelling method.

DEADLY INTERCEPTIONS

The MiG-19S *Farmer-C* did not have to wait long to fire its guns in anger. On March 10, 1964 a USAF RB-66 Destroyer photo reconnaissance aircraft crossed into East German airspace on a mission to observe a military exercise in the Gardelegen training range. It was intercepted by a pair of Russian MiG-19S *Farmer-Cs* from the 24th Air Army based in East Germany and warnings shots were fired and ignored. One of the pilots, Capt Vitaliy Ivannikov was ordered to shoot it down by his ground control intercept facility. The aircraft was downed and the three crewmembers were captured and after intense negotiations by the US president and the Soviet premier, the crew were released after four weeks.

On May 1, 1960 CIA U-2 pilot Francis 'Gary' Powers was shot down by an SA-2 missile over the Soviet Union. In the confusion that followed a pair of MiG-19Ps (all-weather, radar-equipped variants) were told to intercept the last known location of the American aircraft; Russian SA-2 operators on the ground fired and subsequently hit one of the MiG-19Ps, destroying it and killing the pilot.

There were several other incidents during the Cold War involving Soviet or Warsaw Pact forces intercepting Western aircraft and some of these also resulted in losses.

The MiG-19/Shenyang J-6 remains in service in North Korea to this day.

A Pakistan Air Force Shenyang J-6 approaches to land.

Vasily Polyakov's MiG-19 *Farmer* downs RB-47H 53-4281 over international waters on July 1, 1960. Major Palm's body was returned to the USA a month later but the bodies of the three reconnaissance officers were never found. McKone finished his USAF career as a Colonel and received the Legion of Merit with one Oak Leaf Cluster, DFC with one Oak Leaf Cluster and the Prisoner of War Medal. Olmstead also retired as a Colonel having achieved the DFC, Purple Heart and Prisoner of War Medal during his career *Andy Hay / www.flyingart.co.uk*

NOTORIOUS ENCOUNTER

Perhaps the MiG-19's most notorious encounter occurred on July 1, 1960. That afternoon USAF Maj William Palm shepherded his crew to their Boeing RB-47H Stratojet reconnaissance aircraft as they walked out across the concrete apron at RAF Brize Norton, Oxfordshire.

Joining him aboard aircraft 53-4281 would be co-pilot Capt Freeman Bruce Olmstead, navigator Capt John McKone and three reconnaissance officers. Known colloquially as 'Ravens', the recce crew on this day consisted of Maj Eugene Posa, Capt Dean Phillips and Capt Oscar Goforth – the latter making his first operational mission. Their job was to intercept and record the various signals the jet might encounter during its sortie.

The Stratojet and its crew were assigned to the 343th Strategic Reconnaissance Squadron, 55th Strategic Reconnaissance Wing based at Forbes AFB in Kansas but were temporarily flying out of Brize Norton on detachment.

Their mission on July 1 took them northward from the UK where the jet turned east and entered the Barents Sea northeast of Norway. From there, the crew continued over international waters, flying approximately 50 miles from the Soviet Kola Peninsula.

Although there was no intention to enter Soviet airspace, the crew knew the risks. The RB-47 had a relatively low operational ceiling and the Soviet Union had a history of shadowing, escorting and occasionally shooting at American aircraft flying over international waters near its borders.

ROUTINE

There is nothing to suggest the flight was anything but routine until the aircraft reached the Kola Peninsula several hours later. However, a few moments earlier Soviet pilot Vasily Polyakov had strapped into his MiG-19 *Farmer* at Murmansk.

As Polyakov, who was assigned to the 206th Air Division of the Soviet Air Force, climbed out into international waters at the beginning of his sortie it is not known whether he was specifically looking for the RB-47, or whether he too expected a routine day in the cockpit.

The RB-47 crew were flying at 30,000ft (9,144m) and around 425kts (489mph) when they first noticed the MiG was shadowing them at a distance.

As they observed him, Polyakov turned in on an intercept course but passed around three miles behind the RB-47. The crew must have sighed with relief as the radar course now called a turn to the northeast at about 50 miles (80km) off Holy Nose Cape at the bottom of the Kola Peninsula.

However, in the blink of an eye Polyakov's MiG was back – and now he was flying in close formation just 40ft (12m) off the Stratojet's starboard wing. The crew continued with their turn to the northeast (away from the Soviet fighter) and Polyakov broke right as if he was heading back towards Soviet airspace.

Suddenly, without warning the MiG reversed its course and took aim on the Americans before opening fire. Captain Olmstead immediately returned fire, but the RB-47 was no match for the Soviet fighter, which shot up the left wing, engines and fuselage in its initial firing pass.

SPINNING

The Stratojet immediately entered a spin but Major Palm and Captain Olmstead were able to pull out and regain level flight. Then, however, the MiG made a second firing pass and caused further damage.

With the flight crew unable to retain control of the stricken jet, Major Palm gave the order to bail out shortly after 6pm.

At least three of the six crewmen (Olmstead, McKone and Palm) managed to eject but the three Ravens seated in the converted bomb bay were likely unable to get out of the spinning aircraft before it crashed into international waters in the Barents Sea.

Tragically, Major Palm is believed to have died of exposure before he was found but Captains Olmstead and McKone were able to take to their survival rafts. After six hours they were picked up by a Soviet fishing boat.

When later quizzed, the MiG pilot claimed that the combination of internal pressure and his belief that the USAF jet was headed for a secret naval base (which was actually unknown to the USAF crew!) resulted in him shooting down the RB-47, even though it was over international waters in international airspace.

He did not face any charges and on January 24, 1961, after almost seven months of interrogation and prison, Olmstead and McKone were released, having never been brought to trial.

The MiG-19 was the first mass produced and widely exported supersonic fighter in the world. It was a truly incredible design that is not widely known or understood. It served all around the world and served in combat during several conflicts. And yet it still doesn't seem to get the publicity or the respect that it deserves. ❖

The MiG, seen here on October 20, 1953, flew just eleven flight test missions from Okinawa before being shipped to the USA.

Moolah for MiGs
The Quest to 'Buy' a MiG

At the height of the Korean War the USA desperately wanted to get its hands on a serviceable example of the new MiG-15. Steven Taylor looks at a three-year campaign of subterfuge, espionage and good old-fashioned bribery.

When USAF F-80 Shooting Stars tangled with MiG-15s for the first time over the Yalu River on November 8, 1950, not only did it herald a new era in air warfare, as jet versus jet combat became a reality, it also represented a serious threat to the UN forces' control of the airspace over the Korean peninsula, which for the first five months of the Korean War had gone virtually unchallenged.

Although that first jet vs jet battle ended inconclusively (the USAF claimed one MiG-15 destroyed, though Soviet records state that the aircraft was only damaged), it was clear that the unexpected introduction of the new MiG-15 into the conflict threatened to shift the balance of the air war decisively in the Communist forces' favour. Soon, losses of B-29 Superfortress bombers to the MiGs forced the suspension of daylight heavy bombing raids over North Korea.

Naturally, the Western Allies, and in particular the Americans, were anxious to learn as much as they could about the new MiG – many of which were being flown in Korean airspace by Soviet pilots – so they could unlock its secrets and advise UN pilots on the best methods of countering this dangerous new threat. And so began an epic saga that would last almost three years, involving subterfuge, espionage and good-old-fashioned bribery in an attempt to get hold of a MiG-15 fighter.

FISHING FOR A MIG

The first opportunity to acquire a MiG presented itself in July 1951. Early that month, Hawker Sea Furies from the carrier HMS *Glory* spotted a crashed MiG-15 protruding from shallow water off the west coast of North Korea, near Hanch'on. Reconnaissance photographs revealed that the tail section of the MiG had broken off from the fuselage and was lying some distance away. When the find was reported a daring plan for a joint Royal Navy-US Navy salvage operation was quickly set in train.

Recovering the wreckage would, however, be a dangerous undertaking. The downed aircraft was lying in a narrow channel, where the tides were treacherous,

The first opportunity to acquire a MiG presented itself in July 1951 when Hawker Sea Furies from the carrier HMS *Glory* spotted a crashed MiG-15 protruding from shallow water off the west coast of North Korea, near Hanch'on.

some 99 miles (160km) inside enemy territory. The recovery ships would also be exposed to North Korean shore batteries and it was also feared that the southern end of the channel had been mined.

Nevertheless, the chance of seizing even a badly damaged MiG-15 was considered too good to pass up, and a recovery force was hastily assembled, comprising the frigate HMS *Cardigan Bay*, a South Korean launch and a US Navy LCU (Landing Craft Utility) equipped with a crane. Providing air cover throughout the operation would be several 804 Naval Air Sqn Sea Furies flying from *Glory*, with the cruiser HMS *Kenya* providing radar cover to warn of any approaching hostile aircraft.

On July 19, 1951 the LCU was escorted through the tight channel by *Cardigan Bay*, with the Sea Furies flying overhead, keeping a close eye out for any North Korean fighter that might try to attack the ships. "At 1545hrs four Furies were flown off, two to provide cover for the ships already assembled near [the] MiG and two to escort our helicopter (flown by Lieutenant O'Mara of the US Navy) from Chodo Island to the scene of operations," explained the 804 Sqn diary.

"At dead low water," the diary continued, "the body of the MiG was sighted and marked by the helicopter with

> " The chance of seizing even a badly damaged MiG-15 was considered too good to pass up "

a buoy. The tail was marked with a life jacket and dye. The helicopter was then escorted back to Chodo and landed with its tanks pretty empty. The two Furies then went back to the MiG and watched the boats arriving and the activities on the mud whilst the MiG was picked up.

"After three and a half hours the Furies landed on having been relieved by four Corsairs from USS *Sicily*. After refuelling the helicopter arrived back on board the ship and set sail for Kure."

The recovery of the various parts of the MiG-15 was completed without incident and the salvage force escaped safely back through the channel with their prize on the July 21. The wreckage was transported to Inchon before being sent on to the US, where it was analysed at Wright-Patterson AFB in Ohio.

'DENIABLE' MISSIONS

Although the salvaged parts provided valuable information, what was really needed was an intact and flyable example of the fighter, which could be rigorously evaluated in the air by test pilots. To this end, the CIA hatched a daring plan to steal a MiG-15 from an air base behind the Iron Curtain.

The man the Agency selected to carry out this high-risk mission was Jozef Jeka. The Polish pilot, who had escaped to England and joined the RAF in early 1940 after his homeland was overrun by the Nazis, had enjoyed an extremely eventful wartime career, which included spending several months on the run in Occupied France after being shot down in May 1944. Serving mostly with 306 and 316 Sqns, flying first Hurricanes before transferring to Spitfires, he claimed his first enemy kill (a Messerschmitt Me 110) on September 15, 1940. By war's end he was a Squadron Leader and had been awarded the DFM, as well as Polish decorations including the Virtuti Militari and the Cross of Merit.

Jeka's distinguished combat record, coupled with the fact that as a Polish exile he was a stateless citizen, led to his recruitment by the CIA to fly top secret

On March 5, 1953, Polish pilot Franciszek Jarecki defected to the West, landing his MiG-15bis at Ronne Airport on the Danish island of Bornholm. The jet is seen here being examined shortly after arrival. *KEY Collection*

In May 1953 another Polish pilot, Lt Zdzislaw Jazwinski, also defected to Bornholm in his MiG-15. Unfortunately, he made a heavy landing at an army training camp north of Ronne, badly damaging the MiG. *KEY Collection*

Within minutes of landing at Kimpo the MiG-15bis was secured within this hangar to keep it from prying eyes and protect it from attack by North Korean forces.

The earliest known photograph of Lt No's MiG-15bis. Seen parked next to an F-86 at Kimpo Air Base about five minutes after he had landed, this photo was taken without permission from the rear of a passing truck.

'deniable' missions for the Agency during the early years of the Cold War. One of these missions was to steal a MiG-15 by parachuting into Poland, where Jeka would then make his way to an airfield, hijack the aircraft and fly it back to a base in a NATO member state in Western Europe. But an unexpected event overtook the plan before it could be put into action.

DEFECTING TO DENMARK

On March 5, 1953, a fellow Pole, Franciszek Jarecki, defected to the West, landing his MiG-15bis at Ronne Airport on the Danish island of Bornholm. Upon learning of Jarecki's defection, both US and British intelligence were, of course, anxious to examine his aircraft. But the Danes, just as anxious not to antagonise the Soviet bloc, were minded to return the MiG as soon as possible.

A UK Government memo, dated March 10, 1953, revealed: *'[The British Secretary of State for Air] understood that the aircraft was to be handed back on March 16. This gave little time for examination by experts and no opportunity for testing the aircraft's flight capabilities. Moreover, the Danish Government had so far refused permission for any examination of the aircraft by British or American experts.'*

> **" The CIA planned to steal a MiG-15 from behind the Iron Curtain "**

The Danes found themselves caught in the middle of East-West Cold War power politics, as UK and US officials pressed Copenhagen to delay the MiG's repatriation in order that their experts may have the opportunity to closely analyse the aircraft, while the Polish Government stepped up the pressure for its immediate return by harassing Danish fishing boats in the Baltic.

'It might therefore be difficult to persuade the Danes to delay any further the return of the aircraft,' the UK memo pointed out, *'but every effort should be made to induce them to agree that it should first be inspected by British and American experts.'*

These diplomatic efforts bore fruit, for the Danish authorities did indeed grant permission for experts from the Royal Aircraft Establishment and the US Air Technical Intelligence Center to inspect the MiG-15, which had been dismantled and shipped to Copenhagen on March 7. However, requests to conduct flight testing of the MiG were firmly refused by the Danes.

On March 20, the MiG-15 was shipped to Gydnia, Poland, while Jarecki was flown to England by the RAF. He later settled in the US. Two months later another Polish pilot from Jarecki's squadron, Lt Zdzislaw Jazwinski, followed his example and also defected to Bornholm in a MiG-15. Unfortunately, he made a heavy landing at an army training camp north of Ronne, badly damaging the MiG. This aircraft was also examined by British and American experts.

Repainted in USAF markings and insignia, the MiG-15bis under guard and awaiting flight-testing at Okinawa. When it reached Wright-Patterson it was repainted again and was coded TC-616. Rumour has it that the 'TC' stood for test pilot Tom Collins' initials, but as Chuck Yeager was the other main pilot some believe 'TC' stood for "Tom and Chuck"! *All USAF Museum unless stated*

OPERATION *MOOLAH*

The Americans were still desperate to lay their hands on an intact MiG-15 for intensive flight testing, and Jarecki's surprise defection gave them an idea. Less than three weeks after Jarecki's flight to Denmark, the US Joint Chiefs of Staff approved Operation *Moolah* – this was a plan to entice a North Korean MiG-15 pilot to defect to the South by offering political asylum and a reward of $100,000 (almost $1 million in today's money).

In April the offer was broadcast on radio by the commander of UN forces, General Mark Clark, to North Korea and China, his statement promising any defecting pilot 'refuge, protection, humane care and attention', which was transmitted in Russian, Chinese and Mandarin, as well as Korean. When the Communist authorities began jamming the radio transmissions, on the night of April 26, 1953 more than a million leaflets carrying a transcript of General Clark's broadcast were dropped from two B-29s over air bases in North Korea. Further leaflet drops were carried out on May 10 and May 18.

No Communist pilot took up the offer before the signing of the armistice on July 27, 1953 brought an end to the bloody three-year conflict. Two months later, however, a North Korean defector did finally present the Americans with a coveted MiG-15. Shortly before 10.00am on Monday September 21, No Kum-Sok, a Lieutenant in the 2nd Regiment of the Korean People's Air Force, took off from his base at Sunan near Pyongyang on a training flight in his MiG-15bis (serial 2057). Once airborne the 21-year-old pilot set course for Kimpo AB just across the border in South Korea.

Just 17 minutes later Lt Kum-sok's MiG approached the UN base. Fortunately for the defector, no US fighters were

Lt No Kum-Sok's MiG-15bis survives to this day and is on display in the Korean War Gallery at the National Museum of the United States Air Force.

Left: Pictured shortly after his defection in 1953 Lt No Kum-Sok is seen wearing typical Communist flight clothing. Unlike their Western compatriots, MiG-15 pilots did not wear g-suits or hard helmets. **Right:** Lt No Kum-Sok was just 21 years old when he made history and delivered his MiG-15 into Allied hands in 1953.

This leaflet, offering a $100,000 reward to any pilot who delivered a MiG, was dropped on MiG bases in the closing months of the Korean War.

scrambled to intercept the intruder as the base's radar was undergoing routine servicing that morning. In fact, the greatest moment of danger for the Korean airman came as he touched down on the runway and almost collided with a USAF F-86 Sabre, which was also coming in to land on the same runway, from the opposite direction.

Quickly recovering from their initial surprise, the base's guards surrounded the MiG and escorted their Communist guest away for initial questioning. The Lieutenant was then flown by helicopter to the HQ of the 5th Air Force Intelligence at nearby Oryn-dong for a fuller debrief.

PRO-AMERICAN PILOT

For the next six months Lt Kum-sok was intensively interrogated by US Intelligence officers for up to six hours a day, five days a week. The interrogations revealed that No Kum-Sok and his fellow North Korean airmen were unaware of Operation *Moolah's* offer of a $100,000 reward, the MiG-15 squadrons having been pulled back to bases further north at the time of the leaflet drops.

Instead, the pilot's defection was motivated by his secret pro-American views and growing disillusionment with

The MiG takes off from Okinawa for its first flight in Allied hands. An F-86 follows it into the air as a chase plane.

the Communist regime of North Korean leader Kim Il Sung. He was also able to give the Americans a detailed insight into the inner workings of the Korean People's Air Force, including the state of its morale, and revealed the extent of Soviet and Chinese involvement in the Korean Air War.

But the greatest prize was the MiG-15 itself. The aircraft was first taken to Kadena AB in Okinawa where it underwent initial flight testing by, among others, the legendary Major Chuck Yeager. In December 1953, it was carefully dismantled and flown to Wright-Patterson AFB in Ohio for a more extensive evaluation. Overall, the US test pilots felt that the Soviet machine, though possessing a faster climb rate and able to reach a higher ceiling than its nearest US equivalent, the F-86, was let down by its poor handling. A CIA/USAF evaluation also noted that it was not an easy aircraft to escape from in an emergency. 'Bailout from the MiG-15 was feasible only below 700 km/hr [378kts],' they reported.

As for No Kum-Sok, after the CIA and USAF Intelligence had gained every last scrap of intel from their guest, he was granted US residency and awarded his $100,000. Changing his name to Kenneth Rowe, he went on to gain degrees in mechanical and electrical engineering from the University of Delaware, became a US citizen and married a fellow North Korean immigrant, with whom he had three children. After a career working for a number of US defence and aerospace giants including Boeing, Grumman and Westinghouse, he retired to Florida and died on December 26, 2022.

Several more MiG-15 pilots would defect in their aircraft over the following years, both from the Eastern bloc and China, but none had quite the impact of Lieutenant No Kum-Sok's historic flight to freedom on September 21, 1953. ✦

In this doctored photograph of the aircraft, taken in the hangar at Kimpo, the censor has removed the individual '2057' markings from the nose.

SPECIAL MAGAZINES
Essential reading from *Key Publishing*

F-16
The F-16 Fighting Falcon is a multi-role fighter, developed and built in Fort Worth Texas by General Dynamics in the early 1970s and since 1993 by Lockheed Martin.

£9.99 inc FREE P&P*

US AIR FORCES IN EUROPE
Chronicles 80 years of America's flying services.

£8.99 inc FREE P&P*

AIRFORCES OF THE WORLD: EUROPE
This brand-new special publication looks at European air power, country by country and fleet by fleet.

£8.99 inc FREE P&P*

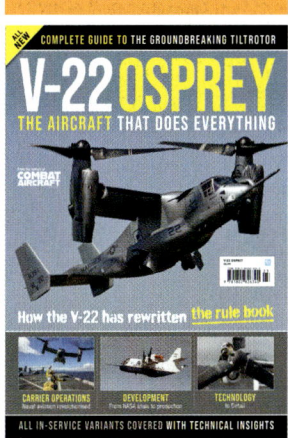

V-22 OSPREY
The Osprey entered US Marine Corps service in 2007 and has since delivered unique capability globally.

£8.99 inc FREE P&P*

F-35
The F-35 is more than an aircraft, but a multi-faceted weapon system in operation with over a dozen different air arms. This eagerly awaited new publication tells that story.

£8.99 inc FREE P&P*

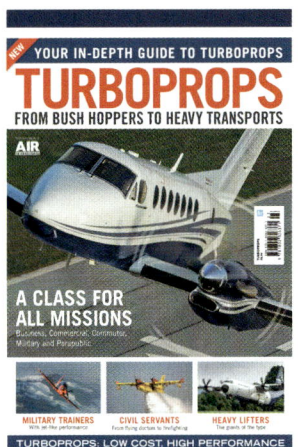

TURBOPROPS
Turboprop aircraft tend to conjure up impressions of twin-engine regional airliners, perhaps epitomised by the ATR family.

£8.99 inc FREE P&P*

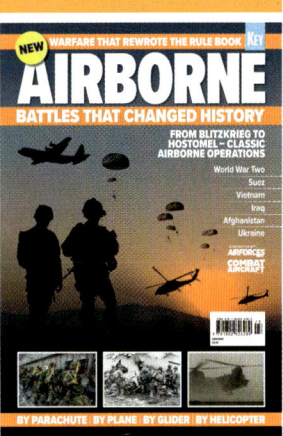

AIRBORNE BATTLES THAT CHANGED HISTORY
This brand new publication looks at the men, the machines, and the missions of these elite fighting men.

£8.99 inc FREE P&P*

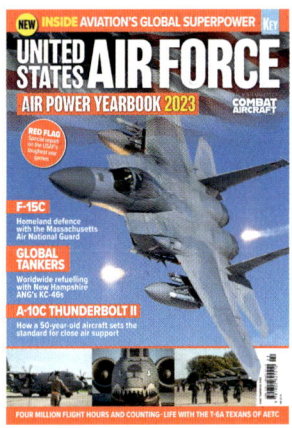

USAF YEARBOOK 2023
Packed with reviews and analysis standing as the ultimate guide to US Air Force air power in 2023.

£8.99 inc FREE P&P*

shop.keypublishing.com/specials

Or call UK: 01780 480404 - Overseas: +44 1780 480404
Monday to Friday 9am–5:30pm GMT.

ALSO AVAILABLE TO DOWNLOAD – search 'Aviation Specials' on Pocketmags.com or your native app store

Free 2nd class P&P on all UK & BFPO orders. Overseas charges apply. All publication dates subject to change.

TO VIEW OUR FULL RANGE OF SPECIALS, VISIT OUR SHOP

Project *Have Doughnut*
DE-CLASSIFIED

A number of MiG-21s have been evaluated at Groom Lake. The type was dubbed the YF-110 in USAF 'service' to avoid admitting it was a captured or 'borrowed' aeroplane.

The emblem of the 4477th Test & Evaluation Squadron.

Documents de-classified in 2014 revealed the extent to which the USAF clandestinely tested a MiG-21 at Groom Lake, Nevada. We trawl through the dossier for nuggets of knowledge

We've long known that the United States secretly tested a captured Mikoyan-Gurevich MiG-21 *Fishbed*, among other Soviet types. We've also known the flying took place at the Groom Lake facility in Nevada (better known by its unofficial title 'Area 51'). But until recently we've not known exactly what the testing entailed and what the US pilots thought of their Soviet nemesis.

Now, thanks to de-classified documents, we can get a glimpse of the project codenamed *Have Doughnut*.

FLYING *FISHBED*
Document FTD-CR-20-13-69-INT, VOL II is dated August 1, 1969 and carries stern warnings that "This report is classified. No foreign dissemination."

Now released into the public domain, the dossier presents the results of a tactical evaluation of a Soviet *Fishbed* E (MiG-21F-13) aircraft and notes that "The exploitation of the MiG-21 aircraft was assigned a high priority since it has been widely exported and deployed to most nations with the communist sphere of influence and is in combat in SEA [South East Asia]."

MISSILE RELIANCE
We now know that the USA has a track record for secretly test flying Soviet Bloc aircraft that dates back to 1953 when the Soviet-built Yakovlev Yak-23 *Flora* was acquired.

In the post-Korean War era the US military was convinced the day of the dogfight was over, and future wars would be won by firing missiles at long distances. Less speculative was the danger of the enemy managing to obtain, understand and reengineer your own missiles.

The infra-red homing AIM-9 *Sidewinder* was America's great wonder weapon in

USAF F-5Es flying with a Soviet Bloc MiG-17 and MiG-21 of the 4477th Tactical Evaluation Squadron sometime in the 1980s. *(All via USAF Museum)*

A YF-110 seen during testing in Nevada.

the late 1950s, but when Taiwanese and Chinese fighters tangled in combat in the Autumn of 1958, disaster occurred. The pilot of a Chinese MiG-17 was hit by an AIM-9B, but the missile failed to detonate and the 'lucky' pilot was able to take it back to his base almost intact.

Another *Sidewinder* allegedly arrived in Moscow in the mail after being stolen from a munitions depot in West Germany and with the Soviets able to reverse engineer the missiles, the tactical advantage was over. The West needed to know how best to counter the Soviet Bloc's fighters.

SOURCING A MIG
The Middle East soon became a prime hunting ground for capturing intact Eastern Bloc aircraft for flight-testing. In 1962, the Soviets began delivering the MiG-21F-13 to several Arab air forces and Israel suddenly found itself under possible threat from this new and very capable fighter. Mossad, the Israeli secret service, immediately began hunting for ways to acquire a *Fishbed* and set about recruiting an Arab pilot who would bring his mount – intact – to Israel.

> **"Mossad began hunting for ways to acquire a *Fishbed*"**

In 1965 a disenchanted Syrian pilot defected to Israel in his MiG-17F and six other pilots followed him in error. The six pilots and three of the seven MiGs were eventually returned to Syria but a year later Mossad got what it wanted when Iraqi pilot Munir Redfa flew his MiG-21 to Israel. The defection, on August 16, 1966, was so well prepared, that Redfa even brought the technical manual with him!

Testing of the MiG proved to be most useful for developing tactics; especially when Israel's forces encountered the *Fishbed* in the Six Day War in 1967.

CHANGE OF ALLEGIANCE
Understandably the Americans were equally keen to get their hands on a MiG-21 and quickly expressed an interest in obtaining Redfa's jet from Israel. However, at this time Israel still maintained good relations with the USSR, which it was reluctant to sully.

Eventually Israel agreed to hand over the MiG-21 to the USA in exchange for

The MiG-17 *Fresco* was tested as part of Project *Have Drill*.

Evaluations found the MiG-21 to have an excellent operational capability in almost all flight regimes, but performance was limited below 15,000ft.

Members of the 4477th Tactical Evaluation Squadron standing in front of a MiG-21 under evaluation.

being allowed to buy the F-4 Phantom II. Israel had made several approaches to the Johnson Administration to purchase the Phantom, only to be rebuffed. But now they had leverage – and in return the US would finally get to study its Vietnam adversary up close.

TESTING TIMES

Very soon Redfa's MiG-21 was on its way to the USA to be followed by at least two Syrian MiG-17F *Frescos* captured by Israelis during the 1967 Six Day War. Their destination was Groom Lake, where they were tested as part of the *Have Doughnut* (MiG-21) and *Have Drill* (MiG-17) programmes.

The first flight out of Groom Lake took place in January 1968 and testing continued until April of that year before the MiG was returned to Israel. During the 102 sorties flown in the USA, the MiG was tested against a variety of fighter and bomber aircraft from the USAF and US Navy.

" The US would finally get to study its Vietnam adversary up close "

COMPARISONS

The de-classified document reveals the findings of the *Have Doughnut* trials and gives an insight into how the US pilots felt about the MiG-21.

The evaluating team believed that the F-4 Phantom II had "the capability to control an engagement" with the MiG-21 below 15,000ft by "orienting the attack towards the *Fishbed's* blind cone in lag pursuit type manoeuvring and by operating in the vertical." The Phantom was also considered to have superior acceleration and could quickly pull away from the *Fishbed*. However, in the turning fight the MiG had "more instantaneous G available than the F-4 at any given airspeed."

Meanwhile, F-105 Thunderchief pilots were told to "press an offensive attack only if an initial rear hemisphere advantage exists. Prolonged manoeuvring engagements should be avoided", was the cautionary advice, as the MiG-21 "has a distinct advantage in turn capability at all airspeeds and altitudes."

However, F-111A and F-100D crews were instructed to "avoid manoeuvring

The Soviet-built MiG-23MS *Flogger-E* was designed for foreign export and was less capable than domestic Soviet versions. This example was acquired by the USAF's 4477th Test Squadron and flew during Project *Constant Peg*. The aircraft was declassified and transferred to the National Museum of the US Air Force in February 2017.

A 4477th Test and Evaluation Squadron MiG-23 marked as Red 49.

engagements with the MiG-21." The Russian jet was considered to have superior acceleration and turn capability.

The F-104 Starfighter was found to be best when employing "high speed, hit and run tactics" and should also avoid prolonged combat; however, it was felt the Northrop F-5 had "considerable potential for engaging the MiG-21 in a tactical situation."

Larger aircraft such as the RF-101 Voodoo and Douglas B-66 Destroyer were both found to be vulnerable to the *Fishbed* and the main theme of the tactic seems to be to 'run away' as quickly as possible! Voodoo crews were advised that the most effective defensive manoeuvre was "maximum power acceleration" with "a steep descent, 45 degrees or more if possible, to provide background IR clutter and increase the acceleration rate."

Destroyer crews were warned their jet was vulnerable to attack from the MiG and "escort protection is mandatory in a high MiG threat area." It was felt the type's survivability "depends upon the escort effectiveness and teamwork. A 3g spiral, considered maximum performance for the B-66, will not negate a MiG-21 missile or gun attack."

CONCLUSIONS

Evaluators noted a number of deficiencies and limitations with the MiG-21, including poor visibility, a weapons system that was "unusable" above 595kts and "extremely poor" engine acceleration. In fact it was said to take 14 seconds to spool up from idle to full military power.

Almost devoid of markings, a USAF YF-110 manoeuvres above the Nevada desert.

Demonstrating the diminutive size of the MiG-21, a pair of 4477th Test Squadron examples return from a simulated combat sortie in company with US Navy F-14 Tomcats.

The canopy of the Shenyang F-7 is hinged at the rear end, unlike that on the MiG-21 which hinges at the front. These two aircraft were in service with the 4477th Test Squadron and wear a rendition of Soviet schemes.

A captured MiG-17 wearing USAF markings during the 1960s.

In conclusion the report notes: "The *Fishbed E* has an excellent operational capability in all flight regimes. However performance is limited below 15,000ft, due to severe airframe buffeting which occurs above 595kts. Heavy longitudinal control forces are encountered at 510kts and above, making high pitch rates difficult or impossible to achieve. Forward visibility through the combining glass, bulletproof slab and windscreen is severely degraded and the rear seat flap, narrow canopy and aircraft structure reduce rearward visibility. Armament is adequate; however, the 30mm cannon is limited to 60 rounds total capacity and considerable pipper jitter occurs during firing. The tracking index drifts off the bottom of the windscreen when tracking targets in excess of 3G. Airspeed bleed-off during high G turns is excessive and engine response is poor."

The Western world learned a lot from Munir Redfa's MiG-21 and the programme of testing clandestinely acquired aircraft continued for some time.

CONSTANT PEG

By the early 1970s the *Have Drill* programme had expanded and a select few US Navy Phantom crews were given the chance to fly against the MiG-17. To prevent any sightings, the airspace above the Groom Lake portion of the Nellis

> "F-111A and F-100D crews were instructed to 'avoid manoeuvring engagements with the MiG-21"

Range was closed. On aeronautical maps, the exercise area was marked in red ink and soon became known as 'Red Square'.

A few years later Vietnam veteran USAF Phantom pilot Colonel Gail Peck suggested a more realistic training programme for his colleagues. During a desk tour at the Department of Defense, Peck had heard about the *Have Drill* and *Have Doughnut* programmes and suggested to USAF General Hoyt S Vandenberg Jr that the captured aircraft be made available to squadron pilots for familiarisation and tactics training. The idea was received favourably and the project code named *Constant Peg* after Vandenberg's callsign ('Constant') and Peck's wife, Peg.

Tactical Air Command therefore established the 4477th Test and Evaluation Flight as a formal USAF unit on April 1, 1977. It began with three MiGs: two MiG-17Fs and a MiG-21 loaned by Israel, who had captured them from the Syrian Air Force and Iraqi Air Force. Later, it added MiG-21s from the Indonesian Air Force and aircraft such as the MiG-23 from other sources.

To disguise their use with the unit the aircraft were given 'experimental' model names with the MiG-21 becoming the YF-110, the MiG-23 referred to as the YF-113 and the MiG-17 classified as the YF-114

A *Have Doughnut* MiG-21 is tested high over Nevada.

for use at Groom Lake.

Whereas the bulk of the MiG's use to date had been as tools with which to understand the performance, capabilities and qualities of the enemy, the 4477th was tasked with training the frontline tactical fighter pilots in how best to fight the Soviet bloc jets. It selected its MiG pilots primarily from the ranks of the Weapons School and Aggressors at Nellis AFB or the Navy Fighter Weapons School.

NEXT GENERATION

By the late 1970s the MiG-17 and MiG-21F had been superseded in Eastern Bloc air arms by later-model MiG-21s and new aircraft, such as the MiG-23.

Fortunately for the USAF, a new source of supply of Soviet aircraft became available in Egypt.

The Soviets had provided the Egyptian air force with MiGs since the mid-1950s but with relations between Egypt and the USSR becoming strained, the Egyptians turned to Western companies for parts to support their late-model MiG-21s and MiG-23s. By way of payment a pair of MiG-23s were given to the USA by Egyptian president Anwar Sadat and shipped to Edwards AFB and, soon afterwards spirited away to Groom Lake for reassembly and study.

A MiG-21 turning final to land at Groom Lake.

Some sources also suggest that the USAF acquired as many as 12 brand-new Shenyang F-7Bs (licence produced MiG-21s) from China in 1987 for use in the *Constant Peg* programme.

Towards the end of the Cold War the programme was ostensibly abandoned and the 4477th squadron was disbanded. Flight operations at Groom Lake and Tonopah allegedly closed down in March 1988, although the 4477th was not de-activated until July 1990. However, although some YF-110/MiG-21s were donated to museums, many of the other aircraft were neither given away nor placed into storage. In fact, the fate of some of them remains classified to this day and others are rumoured to have been buried in the Nevada desert.

ONGOING TESTS

Although the 4477th has long been inactive some of its assets are thought to have been allocated to a detachment of the 57th Fighter Wing at Nellis AFB, now known as Detachment 3, 53rd Test and Evaluation Group.

There have been reports of sightings of the Su-22 *Fitter*, MiG-29 *Fulcrum* and Su-27 *Flanker* flying in the Groom Lake vicinity… but that is an entirely different (and no doubt still very classified) story. ❖

A rare glimpse inside the hangars at Groom Lake reveals a USAF marked MiG-21.

MiG's Fabulous Fishbed

The most-produced supersonic jet aircraft in aviation history and the most-manufactured combat aircraft since the Korean War, the MiG-21 served with more than 60 air arms on four continents and remains in service with more than a dozen nations. Steve Bridgewater looks at the history of this Cold War legend.

The assets of the former Czechoslovak Air Force were divided following the separation of the country into the Czech and Slovak Republics. Slovakia received 21 MiG-21F-13s (actually Czechoslovak-built S-106s), three MiG-21PFs, eleven MiG-21PFMs, eight MiG-21Rs, thirteen MiG-21MA, 36 MiG-12MF, three MiG-21U, two MiG-21US and eleven MiG-21UM airframes. The last few MiG-21UMs still in service were grounded on January 1, 2003. *KEY – Duncan Cubitt*

▲ The Ye-2 was the first of the prototypes to be rolled out and performed its maiden flight on February 14, 1955. It had the AM-9B engine and swept wings.

▶ The Ye-2 was quickly followed into the air by the first Ye-4, which Grigory A Sedov took to the skies on June 16, 1955. This had the delta-wing that would go on to become so familiar on the production variants of the MiG-21.

Left: The Ye-2A had the swept-wing with the new AM-11 powerplant and it performed its initial flight on September 4, 1956.
Right: The Ye-50 prototypes had the swept-wing configuration but the AM-9B powerplant was accompanied by an additional integral liquid-propellant boost engine.

Every Korean War-era pilot wanted an agile fighter and the ability to outfly his opponent in a dogfight. The Americans created the Lockheed F-104 Starfighter and Northrop F-5 Freedom Fighter to fill the role whereas in Europe aircraft as diverse as the Dassault Mirage F1 and Mirage III, English Electric Lightning, Hawker Hunter and Saab Draken joined various NATO air arms.

However, on the other side of the Iron Curtain the USSR had initially concentrated its efforts on the twin-engined MiG-19 (see page 34) but in late 1953 a state requirement for a fast, lightweight fighter was passed down to the aviation industry by the Communist government.

The requirement called for a Mach 2 capable fighter armed with cannon and a radar gunsight. The aircraft must also be able to evolve to accommodate the new era of guided air-to-air missiles (AAMs).

SINGLE UNIT

Although the contract was open to all Soviet design bureaus (OKBs), the MiG OKB effectively won the contract by default as it was the only outfit that had a suitable design and the capacity to develop and build it. The contract was awarded in January 1954.

Mikoyan's design was given the internal codename 'Ye-1' (YE standing for 'Yedinitsa' or 'single unit') and was to be powered by a single Arkady Mikulin AM-5A axial-flow turbojet, but this was quickly dropped in favour of an improved version of the AM-9B already fitted to the MiG-19. Before construction the powerplant was changed yet again, this time to the new Mikulin AM-11, which was in development and being optimised for the fast light fighter requirement. With so many alterations the OKB code for the aircraft was eventually updated to 'Ye-2'. However, the AM-11 was not immediately available so development would have to start using the existing AM-9B to meet the government's deadline.

The actual airframe design was based on studies conducted by the state Central Aerodynamics & Hydrodynamics Institute (known by its Russian acronym TsAGI). For the new aircraft, the TsAGI provided a choice of two configurations – both of which had a slimmer fuselage than the MiG-19 and a conventional tail and mid-mounted wings. However, the designs differed in terms of wing configuration with one design featuring sharply swept-wings similar to the MiG-19 and the other envisioned with a pure delta wing with a leading-edge sweep of 57 degrees.

PROTOTYPES

Uncertainty over which wing configuration to choose and the lack of the proposed engines led the Soviet government to approve the construction of nine prototypes. The Ye-2 would have the swept-wing and AM-9B engine, whereas the Ye-2A had the swept-wing with the new AM-11 powerplant. Also included in the contract were a pair of Ye-4 prototypes (with the delta wing and the AM-9B) and two Ye-5s – the latter having the delta wing and the AM-11 powerplant. Finally, the contract included three Ye-50 prototypes – these machines were to have the swept-wing, an AM-9B engine and an additional integral liquid-propellant boost engine.

The Ye-2 was the first of the prototypes to be rolled out and performed its maiden flight on February 14, 1955 with test pilot Georgiy K Mosolov at the controls. Handling was reported as satisfactory but, as expected, the AM-9B-powered aircraft was underpowered. Nonetheless it was easily capable of reaching Mach 1.8.

The Ye-2 was quickly followed into the air by the first Ye-4, which Grigory A Sedov took to the skies on June 16. To the amazement of the design team the delta-winged Ye-4 was only capable of Mach 1.2 – despite data from the TsAGI suggesting it would be far superior to the swept-wing configuration. The aircraft would need some serious redesigning before it would live up to its full potential but the MiG OKB shared the TsAGI's faith in the concept.

Meanwhile, the new AM-11 powerplant was suffering from severe delays. It was prone to fires and its development repeatedly stalled. As such, it would be January 9, 1956 before Vladimir A Nefyedov took the first delta-winged, AM-11-powered Ye-5 prototype into the skies for the first time. The swept-wing, AM-11-powered Ye-2A prototype performed its initial flight on September 4, 1956 (with Sedov at the controls) and the second Ye-5 finally flew before the end of the year.

INTO PRODUCTION

Trials of the AM-11 powered variants revealed the engine and airframe combination offered great potential. As

The MiG-21F boasted an area-ruled fuselage with an automatically-adjusted moveable intake cone. The triangular wingtips used on the prototypes were changed to cropped tips and the aircraft had a swept all-moving tailplane and a fixed ventral fin. These examples were built in Czechoslovakia as the Aero S-106 but normally referred to as the MiG-21F-13.

Left: Trials of the AM-11 powered variants revealed the engine and airframe combination offered great potential and five Ye-5 pre-production aircraft orders were placed. **Right:** Among the record-breaking MiG-21 variants was the Ye-152. Created to meet the VVS' need for a heavy interceptor to carry out automatic interceptions, MiG developed a range of large fighter aircraft starting with the swept wing I-3 series followed by the I-7 and the I-75. The latter spawned the Ye-152 which was similar in size and configuration to the MiG-21F but twice the weight. Cropped delta wings with greater area allowed the large K-80 or K-9 missiles to be carried on wingtip launchers. The aircraft was powered by a pair of R-15-300 engines but they proved unreliable and flying was limited to evaluation and world record attempts – for which it was referred to as the Ye-166.

Left: The MiG-21PF variant added two fuselage fuel tanks under a fatter rear cockpit fairing. Dubbed the *Fishbed-E* by NATO, the aircraft also had an uprated R-11F2-300 engine that provided 8,710lb/thrust in dry power and 13,490lb/thrust in reheat. **Right:** Scarlet MiG-21PFs of the Red Air Force display team.

such, pre-production batches of five Ye-2A and five Ye-5 aircraft were soon ordered – with the service designation of 'MiG-23' provisionally reserved for the Ye-2A and 'MiG-21' for the Ye-5.

Despite the early problems with the delta wing configuration the 'tweaking' by MiG's design team eventually resulted in the Ye-5 outperforming the swept-wing Ye-2A. It was more manoeuvrable, lighter and slightly faster and the Ye-5/MiG-21 was put into production as the MiG-21. The MiG-23 designation was retired and would be reused a decade later on an entirely different aeroplane.

The first the West knew of the new fighter was when both the swept-wing and delta-winged aircraft appeared in formation at the annual Aviation Day airshow at Tushino Airport in Moscow on June 24, 1956. A series of photographs were leaked by 'friendly faces' in the USSR but these showed nothing more than the general configuration of the aircraft. NATO assigned the swept-wing machine the reporting name of *Faceplate* and the delta-wing machine the name *Fishbed*. It would take a few more years for the West to figure out which one was actually put into production.

Even at this stage the aircraft's configuration was not yet set in stone and in 1957 the engine design bureau, now under the control of Sergei K Tumanskiy, was able to provide a satisfactory version of the AM-11 powerplant. By now the engine had been rebranded as the R-11 with R standing for 'Reaktivniy' (reaction jet engine) and the R-11F-300 offered to the MiG OKB provided a significant increase in power compared to earlier versions – 8,555lb/thrust or 12,655lb/thrust in full reheat.

Three Ye-6 prototypes – combining the now favoured delta-wing with the new R-11F-300 engine – were ordered and the first flew on May 20, 1958 with Vladimir Nefyedov at the controls. It easily exceeded Mach 2 in level flight but the aircraft was lost on May 28 when it suffered a high-altitude flameout. Despite being ordered to eject Nefyedov tried to return the aircraft to base and it crashed onto the runway. He died of his burns in hospital shortly afterwards.

The accident was attributed to the fact that the Ye-6 only had a single hydraulic

The MiG-21PFM *Fishbed-F* introduced a broader tail fin and a new RP-21M radar that linked with a range of radar-guided missiles. Later versions had the KM-1 ejection seat that required a new two-piece canopy, with the glazing hinging open to the right instead of forward.

Yugoslavia purchased its first batch of MiG-21s from the USSR in 1962 and by the early 1980s it had acquired 261 examples in ten variants, including 41 MiG-21F-13s, 36 MiG-21PFMs and 46 MiG-21bis.

The MiG-21bis had the Tumanskiy R-25-300, which provided 9,040lbs of dry thrust and 15,650lb/thrust in afterburner. These are Bulgarian Air Force examples.

A Bulgarian MiG-21bis returns from a training sortie.

Of the 11,496 MiG-21s built, 10,645 of them were produced in the USSR, 657 were manufactured in India and 194 were built in Czechoslovakia. *MiGAvia/Russian Aircraft Corporation*

system so subsequent examples were modified with dual systems. The second Ye-6 flew on September 15 in the hands of Konstantin K Kokkinaki. He concluded that the aircraft could be flown by "any normal pilot" and the go-ahead was given to put the type into production as the MiG-21F. The first deliveries to the VVS took place in late 1959 and the type was given the NATO reporting name *Fishbed-B*.

By this time the mixed-power Ye-50 concept was drawing to a conclusion. The first had flown in June 1956 but only lasted a month before it was written off. The two other examples flew a year later but one was lost following an inflight explosion that killed the test pilot.

The availability of the R-11F-300 powerplant meant there was no real need for rockets and their toxic fuel to be fitted to the aircraft to create extra thrust so the project was officially shelved in late 1957.

RECORD BREAKER

The third Ye-6 was fitted with an upgraded R-11 engine and – designated as the Ye 66 – was used to set speed records. On October 31, 1959 Georgiy Mosolov set a world record over a 25km (15.5 mile) straight-line course of Mach 2.36 (1,556mph).

Another airframe was modified to Ye-66A configuration, with an additional fuel tank behind the cockpit, a redesigned rear cockpit fairing and twin ventral fins. Power came from an uprated R-11F2-300 engine as well as a Dushkin liquid-fuel rocket booster in the belly. On April 28, 1961 Mosolov took the aircraft to a world altitude record of 113,891ft (34,714m).

Both aircraft would go on to achieve a string of records, but the VVS' priorities were geared towards creating a formidable fighter – and the MiG-21F seemed to fit the bill. Constructed mostly of aluminium alloys along with steel, magnesium, and fibreglass, it boasted an area-ruled fuselage with an automatically-adjusted moveable intake cone. The triangular wingtips used on the prototypes were changed to cropped tips and the MiG-21F had a swept all-moving tailplane and a fixed ventral fin. The extreme aft end of the fuselage housed a brake parachute fairing and a hydraulically-actuated airbrake was found below the rear

To produce a two-seater the MiG OKB designers created a 'minimum-change' version of the MiG-21F. The aircraft was exactly the same length as the single-seater and the second seat was crammed in by adjusting the arrangement of internal fuel tanks. The 'twin-stick' MiG-21U *Mongol* first flew on October 17, 1960. This Czech-built example served with the Polish Air Force until 1992 when it was sold to a private owner in Australia, registered VH-XXI and painted in the markings of the Indian Air Force's Red Scorchers. It was retired in 1995 and is now displayed at the Fighter World Museum at RAAF Williamtown.

▲ Large numbers of MiGs were produced under licence in India. Here a HAL-produced MiG-21 joins an Indian Air Force MiG-23, MiG-29, MiG-27 and MiG-25. *Indian Air Force*

◄ The MiG-21's 'office' was painted in the same turquoise applied to most Soviet Bloc aircraft of the period. It is claimed this colour was chosen as it helps to reduce stress and maintain a pilot's effectiveness on long missions.

fuselage. Other airbrakes were situated on the belly.

The delta-wing had a leading-edge sweep of 57 degrees and an anhedral droop of 2 degrees. A single fence prevented loss of airflow over the wingtip.

Armament came in the form of twin 30mm Nudelmann-Richter NR-30 automatic cannons in the belly below the cockpit. The guns were aimed with an ASP-5ND gunsight, which included range gauged by a simple SRD-5 ranging radar. A centreline pylon could accommodate a 108 Imp Gal (490lit) drop tank or a rocket pack. A single pylon below each wing could hold a bomb or unguided rocket pod.

From late 1960 the aircraft was modified to carry an AA-2 *Atoll* air-to-air missile under each wing (albeit at the loss of one of the cannons). Dubbed the MiG-21F-13 *Fishbed-C*, this variant also had an updated SRD-5M Kvant (Quantum) radar.

The MiG-21 proved popular with pilots as it was both fast and agile but as the aircraft evolved it had a tendency to gain weight. With care, an endurance of 90 minutes could be eked out but the aircraft was more of a point-defence interceptor rather than an air defence fighter capable of flying combat air patrol missions.

The handling was far from vice-less though and the small wings resulted in high take-off and landing speeds (and consequently distances). Worse, if the aircraft's angle of attack deviated from its path through the sky, it could disrupt airflow into the intake and cause the engine to quit.

UPGRADED

The MiG-21F was a 'daylight only' fighter and the VVS needed a new version to replace its expensive long-range fighters such as the Yak-25 *Flashlight* and Yak-28P *Firebar*. MiG therefore began work on the Ye-7 prototype, which was effectively a MiG-21F with a Sapfir radar in the nose. The first of eight Ye-7s flew on August 10, 1958 and following trials the type entered production in June 1960 as the MiG-21P (P standing for 'Perekvatchik' or 'Interceptor').

The MiG-21P had provision for two AA-2 *Atoll* missiles but no cannons. It also had redesigned airbrakes and the capability to use rocket-assisted take-off (RATO) boosters. Most notably it had larger tyres in anticipation of future weight increases – these resulting in bulges atop the wing.

By early 1962 the machine was upgraded to MiG-21PF standard. This added two fuselage fuel tanks (as trialled on the Ye-66 project) under a fatter rear cockpit fairing, which boosted

Left: Syrian Air Force MiG-21s have seen service during the nation's recent civil war. The remains of this MiG-21MF are seen at Dhab'a AFB after the Syrian Army retook the base. **Right:** A Hungarian MiG-21bis taxies out for a sortie.

East Germany operated more than 250 MiG-21s including the MiG-21F/F-13, PF, PFM, MF, bis, SPS, U, UM and US variants.

▲ The MiG-21-2000 was a 21st century upgrade offered to export buyers by Israel *Aerospace Industries*.

◀ MiG offered an upgrade package to bring late-model MiG-21s up to the MiG-21-93 standard. This package provides an upgrade of the avionics suite that includes installation of the Kopyo pulse-doppler radar, a smaller version of the N010 Zhuk airborne radar used by the MiG-29, which enables the aircraft to fire a greater range of modern weapons such as the beyond-visual-range Vympel R-77 air-to-air missile. Other upgrade features include installation of a dual-screen HUD, helmet-mounted target designator and advanced flight control systems.

fuel capacity by 605 Imp Gal (2,750 lit). Dubbed the *Fishbed-E* by NATO, the aircraft also had an uprated R-11F2-300 engine that provided 8,710lb/thrust in dry power and 13,490lb/thrust in reheat.

Two years later the MiG-21PFM *Fishbed-F* was introduced; this benefiting from a broader tail fin and a new RP-21M radar that linked with a range of radar-guided missiles. This variant could also be fitted with a 23mm GSh-23 cannon pack on the centreline hard-point and later versions had the KM-1 ejection seat that required a new two-piece canopy, with the glazing hinging open to the right instead of forward.

NEXT GENERATION FISHBED

MiG would go on to produce myriad versions of the fighter. The MiG-21R *Fishbed-H* was a fighter/reconnaissance variant with an enlarged spine. The aircraft could be fitted with a Type D daylight PHOTINT pod, a Type N night-time PHOTINT pod or an Electronic Intelligence (ELINT) pod. In the air-to-air role, the MiG-21R could carry two RS-2US or R-3S missiles and it could also be loaded with bombs or rockets for the strike role.

The MiG-21S *Fishbed-J* was based on the MiG-21PFM but fitted with a new RP-22 radar and ASP-PF-21 computing gunsight. The AP-155 autopilot also featured a 'panic button' auto-recovery system. A MiG-21N variant of the *Fishbed-J* could carry a single RN-25 tactical nuclear weapon.

By the 1970s the MiG-21 had evolved a long way; MiG OKB engineers kept working on the basic design and the MiG-21R formed the basis for what would become the Third Generation *Fishbed*.

By now the bulged spine raised the total fuel capacity to 649 Imp Gal (2,950lit) but resulted in a distinctive humpback appearance. The MiG-21SMT went into production at Gorkiy in 1971 and also benefited from the latest avionics and R-13-300 engine. However, problems with the spine-mounted fuel tanks (much of the fuel was unusable as burning it changed the aircraft's balance and made it unstable) meant a new version was soon on the drawing board.

The latest variant was significantly heavier than its predecessors so the boffins at MiG also needed to source a more powerful engine. The next MiG-21 therefore had the Tumanskiy R-25-300, which provided 9,040lbs of dry thrust and 15,650lb/thrust in afterburner. The new aircraft was dubbed the MiG-21bis ('bis' from the Latin for 'Second') and was a true third generation machine. The aircraft also had an enlarged spine – albeit not as

Among the current MiG-21 operators is North Korea, which is believed to have around 25 examples in service.

Left: Finland was the first country outside the Warsaw Pact to buy the MiG-21, after it had rejected the MiG-19. The Finnish Air Force operated the MiG-21 from 1974 until 1998. **Right:** The MiG-21 LanceR was an upgraded version for the Romanian Air Force produced by Elbit Systems of Israel and Aerostar SA of Romania between 1995 and 2002. The LanceR A version is optimised for ground attack missions and was able to deliver precision guided munitions. The LanceR B, shown here, is the trainer version.

pronounced as the 'SMT. The internal fuel capacity was now 634 Imp Gal (2,880lit) but at least all of it was now usable.

In terms of avionics the new generation of *Fishbed* had an improved RP-22 radar that provided look-down capability to spot low-flying aircraft and an RSBN-6S short-range navigation system and instrument landing system that enabled operation in poor weather. It was armed with the usual GSh-23L cannon and unguided air-to-ground stores but now benefited from new short-range heat-seeking K-60/R-60 missiles (known to NATO as the AA-8 *Aphid*). A total of 2,030 MiG-21bis were built between 1972 and 1984 and the variant was exported widely.

TWIN-STICKER

When the MiG-21F was introduced the main jet conversion trainer in the VVS was the MiG-15UTI *Midget*– which bore zero resemblance to the Mach 2 capable *Fishbed!* To produce a two-seater the MiG OKB designers created a 'minimum-change' version of MiG-21F-13. The aircraft was exactly the same length as the single-seater and the second seat was crammed in by adjusting the arrangement of internal fuel tanks, and by deleting the cannon the jet was able to retain the same fuel capacity as the MiG-21F-13. The downside of this was that the instructor's position in the rear was not raised, giving him a poor forward view. The 'twin-sticker' could carry an AA-2 *Atoll* missile under each wing and a 12.7mm machine gun could be fitted into a centreline pod.

The first of the two Ye-6U prototypes (later referred to as MiG-21U with U standing for 'Uchyebniy' or Trainer) performed its maiden flight on October 17, 1960.

Subsequent production versions of the MiG-21U for the VVS were built at State Factory 31 in Tbilisi, Georgia and examples for export were built at the Znamya Truda factory near Moscow. NATO assigned it the reporting name *Mongol*.

China's Chengdu Aircraft Company produces a version of the MiG-21C called the J-7 and in 2009 Pakistan started to produce the type under licence as the JF-17. The new variant features a glass cockpit, a fly-by-wire flight control system and 'Hands On Throttle-And-Stick' (HOTAS) controls and remains in production to this day.

CHINESE 'COPY'

In early 1961 Communist China entered into an agreement with the MiG OKB to build the MiG-21 under licence. The state factory at Shenyang was to produce the jets but relations between the two nations broke down before all of the necessary parts and information had been delivered.

Eventually, the Chinese ended up building the aircraft without Soviet assistance, designating it the CAC (Chengdu Aircraft Company) J-7. The first example flew on January 17, 1966 with test pilot Ge Wenrong at the controls. After

FISHBEDS IN COMBAT

Although the MiG-21 never saw combat during the Cold War, the type was stationed in Cuba during the October 1962 Missile Crisis. The type would see extensive active service elsewhere in the world beginning in 1965 when Indian examples tangled with Pakistani fighters (albeit without a victory). Two years later Egyptian aircraft shot down a pair of Israeli Dassault Super Mystères to claim the MiG-21's first scalps.

During the Six Day War an Iraqi MiG-21F-13 damaged an Israeli Mirage IIICJ but more than 120 MiG-21s were destroyed on the ground and in the air. In 1971 Indian Air Force *Fishbeds* downed three Pakistani F-104s but it was during the Vietnam War that the MiG really got its first taste of large scale combat, with the North Vietnamese Air Force claiming 103 US F-4 Phantoms shot down by MiG-21s – at the cost of 60 *Fishbeds*. Interestingly, only 47 of the MiG claims have been definitely confirmed.

During the 1967-1973 War of Attrition between the Israelis and Arabs, Syrian MiG-21s claimed 13 kills against Israeli fighters and Egyptian aircraft claimed a further 17 victories. However, around 100 Arab MiG-21s are thought to have been shot down by the Israelis.

At least one Egyptian MiG-21 was also shot down during the 1977 conflict between Libya and Egypt but in 1979 an Egyptian MiG-21 downed a Libyan MiG-23MS.

During Angola's long-running civil war a number of MiG-21s were lost in combat with South African Mirage F1s.

In the 1977–78 Ogaden War, Ethiopian Air Force F-5As and MiG-21MFs engaged Somali Air Force MiG-21MFs in combat on several occasions. Ethiopia claimed to have shot down ten Somali MiG-21MFs; while Somalia also claimed to have destroyed several Ethiopian MiG-21MFs.

In different Israeli–Syrian clashes, between 1979 and 1981, at least a dozen MiG-21s were shot down, for no gains in exchange. In 1982, Israel claimed up to 25 Syrian MiG-21s downed.

During the Iran–Iraq War (1980–1988), a total of 23 Iraqi MiG-21s were shot down by Iranian F-14s and 29 more fell to Iranian F-4 Phantoms. However, Iraqi MiG-21s shot down 43 Iranian fighter aircraft in the same period.

In more recent years MiG-21s have been involved in the 1991-1995 Yugoslavian Wars and records indicate at least seven MiG-21s were shot down by ground fire in Croatia and Bosnia.

During the 1991 Gulf War two Iraqi J-7Bs (Chinese versions of the MiG-21F-13s) were shot down by US Navy F/A-18 Hornets and in the on-going Syrian Civil War at least three MiG-21s have been lost to ground fire. The type also saw limited service in the 2011 Libyan Civil War but the only losses are thought to have been caused by pilot error.

Records suggest that throughout its lifetime the MiG-21 has scored 240 air-to-air victories – albeit at a cost of 501 air-to-air losses to its opponents. During that time several pilots have attained ace status (five or more aerial victories/kills) while flying the type, with North Vietnamese Air Force Captain Nguyễn Văn Cốc regarded as the most successful with nine kills. Twelve other NVAF pilots achieved ace status and three Syrian pilots also reached the milestone – all three during the 1973–1974 engagements against Israel. Other high scorers include Iraqi pilot S A Razak and Egyptian pilot A Wafai – each with four victories to their name.

During the Vietnam War the MiG got its first taste of large scale combat, with the North Vietnamese Air Force claiming 103 US F-4 Phantoms shot down by MiG-21s – at the cost of 60 Fishbeds. Interestingly, only 47 of the MiG claims have been definitely confirmed. This MiG-21PF wears Vietnam People's Air Force markings and is exhibited at the National Museum of the United States Air Force. USAF Museum

extended testing the J-7I production version was finally airborne by June 1976. Although it was only built in small numbers the type was exported to Albania and Tanzania.

A much-improved J-7B flew in December 1978 and was fitted with a more reliable WP-7B engine and better ejection seat. As well as service in China, the variant was exported as the F-7B to Egypt, Iraq, and Sri Lanka.

The aircraft continued to evolve and more modern versions appealed to air forces on a budget – such as those of Bangladesh, Egypt, Iran, Myanmar, Pakistan and Zimbabwe. A two-seat version (the JJ-7) was also produced from 1985 and in 2009 Pakistan started to produce the JF-17 version of the single-seater under licence.

The JF-17 features a glass cockpit, a fly-by-wire flight control system and 'Hands On Throttle And Stick' (HOTAS) controls and remains in production to this day.

EXPORT MARKET

The MiG-21 had obvious export potential and the first example was sold to Czechoslovakia in 1960 – it would go on to serve with around 60 nations on four continents. The aircraft was also built extensively overseas, with the Czech Aero Vodochody factory in Prague being the first to obtain a license to build the type. The Czechs built 194 examples of the MiG-21F (as the S-106).

Export machines generally had systems built to a slightly lower standard than Soviet examples but North Vietnam obtained a unique tropicalised variant of the MiG-21PF (the MiG-21PF-V), with systems tuned for high temperature and humidity. Hindustan Aircraft Ltd (HAL) in India also licence-built a downgraded version of the MiG-21PFM as the MiG-21FL.

While the USSR was by far the largest user of the MiG-21 (operating more than 6,000 examples), almost every Eastern Bloc nation from Albania to Yugoslavia also flew the type. Finland was the only Western European nation to obtain the *Fishbed*, obtaining 61 examples of the MiG-21F-13, the MiG-21bis, and the MiG-21U/UM. Meanwhile, users in North Africa and the Middle East included Algeria, Egypt, Iraq, Libya, Syria, Syria, and Yemen. Elsewhere in Africa the type was flown extensively in countries as diverse as Ethiopia, Mozambique, Nigeria and Sudan. Users to a lesser degree included Burkino Faso (previously Upper Volta), the Congo, Guinea Malgasy, Mali, Somalia, and Uganda. In addition to India, other users in South Asia included Afghanistan, Bangladesh, and Sri Lanka. In East Asia the MiG-21 has flown with the air arms of Cambodia, Indonesia, Laos, Mongolia, North Korea, and North Vietnam.

Elsewhere across the globe the *Fishbed* flew with the Cubans and several examples were acquired by the USA for evaluation and to fly as 'aggressors' in military exercises.

By the end of the Cold War, and the collapse of the Soviet Union in the early 1990s, the MiG-21 was already well beyond its best and had been replaced in VVS service by the superior MiG-29 and Sukhoi Su-27. However, it had cemented its role in history with a total of 11,496 produced, and today – nearly 70 years after the Ye-2 first flew – the *Fishbed* remains in operational service with the air arms of Croatia, Cuba, Egypt, India, Libya, Mali, Mozambique, North Korea, Romania, Serbia, Syria, Uganda and Zambia. ❖

Mikoyan-Gurevich MiG-21MF *Fishbed-J* in Detail

The Mikoyan-Gurevich MiG-21MF (M standing for Modernizirovannyy or 'Modernised' and the F relating to the word Forsirovannyy, which translates into 'Uprated' and refers to the engine) was the export version of the Russian Air Force's MiG-21SM variant. The aircraft differed slightly in that it had RP-22 radar and the R13-300 turbojet. The choice of weapons loads was also increased slightly with the addition of the R-60 (NATO: AA-8 *Aphid*) and later the R-60M IR-seeking AAM. The type received the NATO reporting name *Fishbed J* and was also licence-built in India by HAL as the Type 88.

The MF variant served extensively with nations as diverse as Cuba (60 delivered from 1972), Egypt (110 airframes), Libya, Mali, North Korea, Romania, Syria and Uganda.

KEY

1. Glassfibre radome, fore-and-aft moveable
2. Angle of attack probe
3. Steel intake lip
4. Pitot head
5. Boundary layer bleed duct
6. Boundary layer exit (top and bottom)
7. Divided intake ducting
8. Suction relief door
9. Suction relief door
10. Nosewheel debris deflector
11. 'Spin-scan' fire control radar
12. Avionics compartment
13. Dynamic pressure probe unit
14. Canopy
15. Rear view mirror
16. Radar display and electronic sighting unit
17. Pilot's 'zero-zero' ejector seat
18. Control stick
19. Rudder pedals
20. Throttle quadrant
21. Fore and aft armoured bulkheads, aft with ejector seat rails
22. Electrical equipment bay
23. SPA-10 Sirena radar equipment
24. Communications equipment
25. Fuel system gravity tank
26. Fuselage bag-type fuel tanks
27. Glassfibre top decking
28. Fuel filler and recuperator
29. Control runs to rear fuselage
30. Wing main box section spars
31. Outer auxiliary spars
32. Auxiliary spars
33. 108gal drop tank
34. Inward retracting mainwheel leg with pneumatic brakes
35. Leg actuator/main strut
36. Mainwheel stowage
37. Forward-retracting steerable nosewheel.
38. Bolted aft fuselage joint (for engine removal)
39. Tumansky RD-13-300 turbojet
40. Engine oil tank
41. Hydraulic accumulator
42. Jet exit
43. External nozzle actuator duct
44. Spare/fuselage frame pin joints
45. Engine bay venting intake
46. All-moving tailplane
47. Anti-flutter weight
48. Tailplane actuator
49. Tailplane control hydraulic pack
50. Rudder actuator
51. Aileron jack
52. 'Blown' flaps.
53. Flap actuator
54. Flap hinge
55. Ventral fin
56. Airbrakes (each side)
57. Brake parachute stowage
58. Retractable landing/taxiing lamp
59. IFF antenna (on fin and under intake)
60. VHF aerial
61. UHF antenna
62. Fuel vent
63. Twin-barrel 23mm Gsh-23 cannon
64. K-13A *Atoll* air-to-air missile
65. UV-16-57 rocket pack (16 x 57mm rockets)

SPECIFICATION
MIKOYAN-GUREVICH MiG-21MF

Crew	1
Length	51ft 9in (15.76m)
Wingspan	23ft 6in (7.15m)
Height	14ft 9in (4.50m)
Wing Area	247.6ft² (23.00m²)
Empty Weight	12,544lbs (5,690kg)
Loaded Weight	21,764lbs (9,872kg)
Max Speed	(Sea Level) Mach 1.05 (808mph/1,300km/h)
Max Speed	(at 42,000ft) Mach 1.76 (1,351mph/2,176km/h)
Service Ceiling	58,070ft (17,700m)
Combat Range	1,118 miles (1,799km)
Powerplant:	One 9,040lb/thrust (14,550lb/thrust in afterburner) Tumansky R-13-300 afterburning turbojet
Armament	One GSh-23 cannon plus a variety of air-to-air and air-to-ground missiles including the S-5, S-24, Kh-66, RS-2US, R-13M, R-60, R60M and freefall bombs.

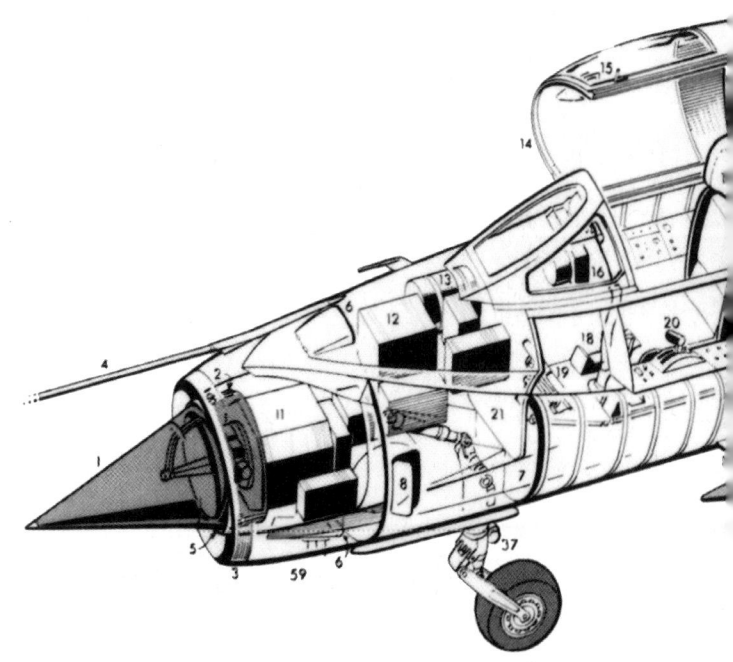

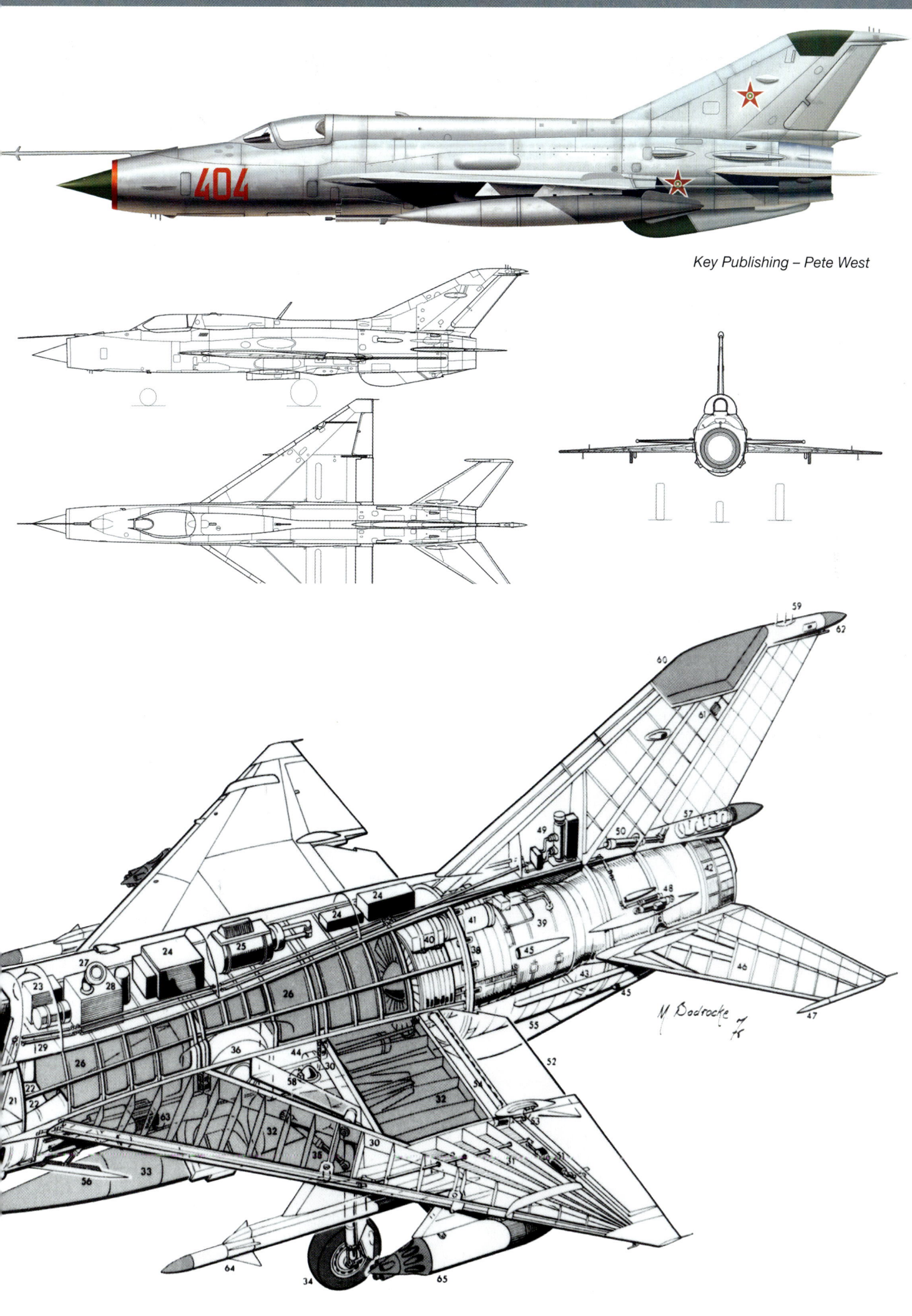

Key Publishing – Pete West

Swing-Wing MiGs

Deliveries of MiG-23MS and MiG-23UB airframes to Syria began on October 14, 1973 and the type saw operational frontline use including four combat missions over Lebanon. Much more recently, examples have participated in the Syrian civil war.

Among the most distinctive of all MiG jets were the variable-geometry MiG-23 and MiG-27 *Floggers*. Paul Fiddian discusses the development and operational history of the fighter-bomber and ground attack variants

Staged on July 9, 1967 to mark the 50th anniversary of the October Revolution, the Domodedovo airshow was the Soviet Union's first event in six years. Alongside the mass formations and tactical demonstrations came a wealth of public debuts, among them two new MiG models of which one had, at that point, been flying for less than a month.

The Mikoyan-Gurevich MiG-23 was initially conceived as a replacement for the MiG-21 that would deliver several levels of improvement – greater range, more advanced avionics and a new-generation weapons-launching capability all being sought. Given the MiG-21's extended runway need, an enhanced take-off performance was one key requirement – with increased deployability would come increased tactical capability – as was increased speed and stability within the low-level arena. Mikoyan had two approaches in mind: additional thrust and 'swing-wing' technology and, using separate airframes, put both to the test.

LIFT JETS

The MiG OKB's 23-01 was the first to fly, on April 3, 1967. Featuring upsized MiG-21 wings, it also had two Koliesev lift jets supplementing the main 22,046lb/thrust Lyulka AL-7F turbojet to improve take-off performance. These lift jets were positioned vertically in the fuselage's underside, right where the aircraft's centre of gravity was sited. Lateral intakes – one on each fuselage side – fed the primary powerplant, a dorsal intake doing the same for the lift engines. After take-off, the novel thrust providers contributed nothing but unnecessary weight and, for that reason, development of the 23-01 ended.

> **" Wing swing process took approximately 15 seconds from one extreme to the other "**

Rather than lift jets, the 23-11 (later the Ye-231) incorporated variable-geometry wings that moved through 56 degrees of sweep. The wing was angled for 16 degrees off the horizontal when sat fully forward and reached 72 degrees at full sweep, via a 45-degree midpoint. In turn this took the 23-11's wingspan from 45ft 10in (13.97m) to 25ft 6in (7.77m). The swing-back process was pilot-induced, enabled by well-separated hinge points and lasted approximately 15 seconds to travel from one extreme to the other.

Under test pilot Alexander Vasilevich Fedotov's command, the 23-11 prototype had its maiden flight on June 10, 1967. This was the first of nine prototypes, including two static test platforms. In December of that year approval to initiate full production was received.

FIRST *FLOGGER*

Designated MiG-23S (and given the NATO reporting name *Flogger-A*), the first production airframe lifted off on May 23, 1969, with Fedotov once more in the cockpit.

Full operational capability in Soviet Air Force service was reached during 1971 and while MiG-23S manufacturing ran to a little over 60 examples the type didn't, in its earliest form, quite meet expectations.

Development of its intended Sapfir-23 radar was running behind schedule, so the earlier-generation S-21 weapons control system stood-in. With just 11 miles (18km) of radar coverage possible and a limited weapons load (one 23mm GSh-23 cannon plus four Vympel K-13 short-range air-to-air missiles) in place, the MiG-23S was under-armed and also not all-weather-capable. The aircraft therefore never progressed beyond the operational testing stage and those airframes delivered were relegated to training duties.

Joining the Soviet Air Force just months later, the follow-up MiG-23SM (sometimes referred to as the MiG-23 Type 1971) was a significant improvement. Now fully operational and integrated with the airframe the S-23 weapons suite combined the Sapfir-23 radar and the brand-new medium-range Vympel R-23R missile (AA-7 *Apex*).

Various structural modifications were also performed including a wing reset that added 2.5 degrees to each

Left: The MiG 23-01 featured upsized MiG-21 wings and two Koliesev lift jets supplementing the main 22,046lb/thrust Lyulka AL-7F turbojet to improve take-off performance. These lift jets were positioned vertically in the fuselage's underside, right where the aircraft's centre of gravity was sited. After take-off, the novel thrust providers contributed nothing but unnecessary weight and, for that reason, development of the 23-01 ended. **Right:** The second MiG proposal for the contract was the MiG 23-11 (or Ye-231), which featured variable-geometry wings.

◀ The MiG-23's full operational capability in Soviet Air Force service was reached during 1971.

▶ The MiG-23M also added the new Sapfir-23D radar, able to pick out *Flogger*-sized targets across 30 miles of sky.

position. Around 80 MiG-23SMs were manufactured but mass production eluded the type until the advent of the MiG-23M in June 1972. This variant introduced a primitive look-down/shoot-down capability to both the *Flogger* and the Soviet Air Force at large.

The MiG-23M also added the new Sapfir-23D radar, able to pick out *Flogger*-sized targets across 30 miles (45km) of sky and the type was manufactured in large quantities: 1,300-plus leaving the factory lines between 1972 and 1977.

Its engine, a Tumansky R-29B, generated 27,500lb/thrust and this, combined with the now-standard Sapfir-23D, PT-23 IRST (infrared search and track) sensor and ASP-23D gunsight created a potent ground attack machine. It was so good, in fact, that a specialised ground attack version, the MiG-27, was envisaged – more of which anon.

EXPORT MARKET

Two MiG-23M models, the MF and MS, were created for the export market. Warsaw Pact states got the MF – its specifications closely-matching the Ms. Featuring simplified avionics and compatible with only short-range missiles, the MS was for non-Eastern European nations but didn't prove too popular. The MF's sales market thus became more international than intended but the airframes supplied still had intentionally downgraded systems, keeping its full mission capability within the Warsaw Pact.

By the mid-1980s, frontline Soviet Air Force squadrons had converted from the MiG-23M to the next model: the MiG-23ML. The MiG-23Ms were either exported, put in 'live' storage or – as had their forebears – retasked as trainers. Modernised avionics and a stream of other advances – integration of the AA-10 *Alamo* and AA11 *Archer* missiles' among the latter – were among this model's contribution to the *Flogger* legacy.

Lighter than its predecessors, the MiG-23ML lost the distinctive nose-high stance they adopted at ground level. Upgraded to S-23ML standard, its avionics included the Sapfir-23ML radar that delivered both improved reliability and a 65km (40 miles) range. Further radar improvements and the addition of Vympel R-24R/T missile created the MiG-23MLA sub-variant.

Around 1,100 MiG-23MLs and MLAs were manufactured and, once again, Warsaw Pact and non-Warsaw Pact member countries were given essentially like-for-like and slightly weakened examples, respectively.

Just over 560 MLs/MLAs were upgraded to the MLD standard that brought the *Flogger* series to a close. Almost two decades' of evolution had produced a new-generation *Flogger* to meet a new decade's challenges. Equipped with Sapfir-23MLA-II radar and Vympel R-73 missiles, the jet was also the most agile MiG-23 yet, thanks in no small part to saw-toothed wing roots.

An East German MiG-23 lands back after a training sortie. Following the reunification of Germany, the German Air Force gave two MiG-23s to the USAF and one to a museum in Florida, the others were given away to others states or scrapped.

More than 5,000 MiG-23s were built with large numbers serving with the Soviet Air Force.

Left: The prototype MiG-23 first flew on June 10, 1967 and can now be found at the Central Air Force Museum at Monino outside Moscow. *Steve Bridgewater* **Right:** A Polish Air Force MiG-23 blasts into the sky at the start of a sortie.

AIR DEFENCE *FLOGGER*

In between the ML and MLD came the MiG-23P, which specialised in air defence. Harnessing the ML's airframe and engine, its revisions included a modified fin root. Approximately 500 were built during 1978–1981 and they equipped solely the Soviet Air Defence Forces. The model notably served in an aggressor role early in its career, in which capacity it played the 'enemy' for the benefit of MiG-29 students. Outside of dogfighting scenarios, where the newer type excelled, the most experienced MiG-23P pilots found they could 'defeat' their opponents with a 'hit-and-run' approach. The 'P' remained in service until 1998, thereby bringing Soviet military type use to an end.

Type conversion had not been an easy process and in 1973 a dedicated two-seat trainer version – the MiG-23U – joined the range. Based on the MiG-23S, the jet featured a second cockpit in an elevated position behind the original. To enable this modification a fuel tank needed relocating further back in the fuselage. Systemic alterations were also carried out to make the MiG-23U a dual ground attack and air-to-air combat training platform. Loaded with AA-2 *Atolls* or A-8 *Aphids*, it had a corresponding combat capability. The initial Tumansky R-27 in time gave way to the R-29, creating the UB sub-variant and, similarly, MiG-23M wings were fed in at the mid-late production stage. A total of 769 training *Floggers* – a mixture of conversions and new-builds – were manufactured.

By the time MiG-23 production finished a total of 5,047 examples had been built. Of these, more than 200 remain in service with ten nations including Angola (that has 22), the Democratic Republic of the Congo (two), Ethiopia (7), Kazakhstan (three), Libya (up to five), North Korea (56), Sudan (three) and Zimbabwe (three).

Syria has been the primary Flogger user in recent years, with 89 airframes before the nation's civil war. Deliveries of MiG-23MS and MiG-23UB airframes to Syria began on October 14, 1973 and the type has seen extensive operational frontline use including four combat missions over Lebanon. Much more recently, examples have participated in the Syrian civil war.

ATTACK *FLOGGER*

As previously mentioned, the potential for the MiG-23M to be used in the ground-attack role was not lost on the engineers at the MiG OKB.

By the late 1960s the VVS' primary attack aircraft was the MiG-17, which had been built as an air-superiority fighter but shifted to the attack role later in its life. These were aided by limited numbers of Sukhoi Su-7B airframes – the USSR's first production purpose-built jet attack aircraft. The Su-7 had a poor warload and range and many pilots claimed the MiG-17 was a more effective strike aircraft.

A state requirement was therefore issued for a new jet attack aircraft, with proposals from the Sukhoi and Mikoyan OKBs selected from a wide range of submissions.

Sukhoi offered the Su-17, which was essentially a much improved, version of the Su-7B with variable geometry wings and MiG OKB decided the quickest and cheapest way of meeting the requirement would be to modify the *Flogger* into the MiG-23Sh variant – with 'Sh' standing for 'Shturmovik' or 'Storm Bird'; the name traditionally given to Soviet ground attack aircraft.

One of the MiG 23-11 prototypes was reactivated and modified to carry bombs on four pylons. The aircraft didn't perform very well, but the exercise highlighted areas for improvement.

A mock-up of the new aircraft was presented to air force officials in 1969 and early the following year approval was given to begin developing a flyable prototype. Initially dubbed the MiG-23B (B for 'bombardirovshtik' or bomber) and referred to by NATO as the *Flogger-F*, the new aircraft had an improved field of view

Up to five MiG-23s were thought to remain in service with the Libyan Air Force in 2018.

The MiG-23 equipped the Soviet Air Force until 1998.

from the cockpit, stronger landing gear and increased thrust from a 24,700lb/ thrust Lyulka AL-21F-300 engine.

With Fedotov at the controls once again the new aircraft flew for the first time on February 18, 1971.

ARMOURED JET

The new aircraft featured an armoured glass canopy and steel armour panels alongside the cockpit. Thick aluminium belly panels also protected the engine and the fuel tanks featured an inert gas system to prevent ignition if the tanks were hit.

Within the cockpit the pilot had access to a Sokol-23S navigation-attack system (which integrated with a laser rangefinder/ marked target seeker system in the nose), an ASP-17 reflector sight and a PBK-3 toss-bombing sight. A Doppler radar, radar altimeter, radio direction finder and radio navigation system receiver were also fitted and the navigation system was linked to the autopilot, enabling it to follow a pre-programmed attack route. In terms of self-defence the jet had a Siren-FSh radio frequency (RF) jammer and a Sirena-10M radar warning receiver.

Weaponry included the original GSh-23L twin-barrelled cannon as well as an extra set of stores attachments on the rear fuselage that could carry 550lb (250kg) bombs or a rocket-assisted take-off pack. In total the jet could carry 6,614lbs (3,000kg) of external stores and was typically loaded with a mixture of bombs and rockets. Cannon pods could also be carried on the wing glove pylons and four R-60 / AA-8 *Aphid* air-to-air missiles could be carried for self-defence.

The prototype MiG-23B flew for the first time on February 18, 1971.

Only 24 MiG-23Bs were built and they were mostly used as evaluation aircraft. Eventually production switched to the upgraded MiG-23BN *Flogger-H*, which was powered by the 23,370lb/ thrust R29B-300 engine. This offered commonality with the MiG-23MS and MiG-23MF fighter variants already sold to the rest of world and also had the benefit of being specifically designed for low-level subsonic flight.

Compared to earlier aircraft the MiG-23BN had a revised nose – nicknamed 'Utkonos' (Platypus) in Russian service. The downward-sloping profile improved pilot visibility and among its test pilots it was also called 'Balkon' (Balcony) because of the increased frontal view from the cockpit.

A total of 624 MiG-23BNs were built with most being exported to Warsaw Pact countries such as Bulgaria, Czechoslovakia, and East Germany and other 'sympathetic' nations including Algeria, Cuba, Egypt, Ethiopia, India, Iraq, Libya, and Syria. Of these, some of the largest operators were India (95 examples) and Iraq (80) – the latter retrofitting them with an aerial refuelling capability.

MIG-27

The VVS only obtained 100 MiG-23BNs because it soon realised the next variant – the MiG-23BM was to be a far superior airframe. In fact the airframe was so different from its predecessor that it warranted a new designation and the MiG-27 was born.

Retaining the R-29B-300 engine, the MiG-27 dispensed with the variable engine intake ramps in favour of a splitter plate that prevented the ingestion of turbulent and stagnant boundary layer air that hugged the fuselage. Top speed fell to Mach 1.7 but the resultant 660lbs (300kg) reduction in weight was considered more valuable. The landing gear was also strengthened and the pylons upgraded to allow a maximum external load of 8,800lbs (4,000kg). Additional cockpit armour was installed along with a totally new nav/attack system and the two barrelled GSh-23L cannon was swapped for a 30mm six-barrelled Gatling-type GSh-6-30 gun, with a rate of fire of 5,000 rounds per minute.

The prototype MiG-27 flew for the first time on November 17, 1972 with test pilot Valeriy Menitskiy at the controls.

Left: Red 12 demonstrates the MiG-23's wings in their fully forward – 16 degree – position. **Right:** In 1973 a dedicated two-seat trainer version – the MiG-23U – joined the range. Based on the MiG-23S, the jet featured a second cockpit in an elevated position behind the original. This is a Czech Air Force example.

Only 24 MiG-23Bs were built before production switched to the MiG-23BN. The new type had a revised nose – nicknamed Utkonos (Platypus) in Russian service. A total of 624 MiG-23BNs were built with most being exported to Warsaw Pact countries such as Bulgaria, Czechoslovakia, and East Germany and other 'sympathetic' nations including Algeria, Cuba, Egypt, Ethiopia, India, Iraq, Libya, and Syria. These are Czech examples.

The most obvious difference between the MiG-23 and the MiG-27 is the latter's sloping nose. This improved pilot visibility and among its test pilots it was also called 'Balkon' (Balcony) because of the increased frontal view from the cockpit. This is an East German example.

A Soviet Air Force MiG-27 trails its braking 'chute as it taxies back to the dispersal.

A total of 90 MiG-23s were operated by the Bulgarian Air Force, including 33 MiG-23BNs.

Serial production began in late 1973 at Irkutsk's state factory GAZ-124 in Siberia and the MiG-27 entered VVS service in 1975 – at which time it was given the NATO reporting name *Flogger-D*.

A total of 360 MiG-27s were built before production switched to the MiG-27K variant with a substantially updated avionics suite. The MiG-27K was the most advanced Soviet variant, with a laser designator and compatibility with TV-guided electro-optical weapons. Some 197 were built as the *Flogger-J2*.

Concerns over the complexity of the MiG-27K led to the development of a simpler variant, the MiG-27M, which would receive the reporting name *Flogger-J*. This was cheaper and easier to build than the MiG-27K, but much better than the MiG-23B, MiG-23BN, and MiG-27 (MiG-23BM). It had the electro-optical and radio-frequency feeds above the glove pylons deleted and was armed with the GSh-6-23M Gatling gun. If needed this could be replaced by a 30mm GSh-6-30 six-barrelled cannon in a fuselage gondola.

The MiG-27M also received a much-improved electronic countermeasure (ECM) system, and a new PrNK-23K nav/attack system providing automatic flight control, gun firing, and weapons release. A total of 200 MiG-27Ms were built from 1978 to 1983 and a further 305 MiG-27Ds were later upgraded to MiG-27M standard.

The MiG-27ML was introduced in 1986 as an export variant of the MiG-27M specifically for sale to India. A total of 150 were assembled in India by Hindustan Aircraft Limited, many of which remain operational today.

Left: The MiG-27ML was introduced in 1986 as an export variant of the MiG-27M specifically for sale to India. A total of 150 were assembled in India by Hindustan Aircraft Limited. **Right:** Indian MiG-27s saw extensive combat, especially during the 1999 Kargil War, when one was lost together with a MiG-21 while supporting an Indian ground offensive in the Kashmir region. The Indian Air Force retired its last MiG-27 squadron in December 2019.

SPECIFICATION MIKOYAN-GUREVICH MIG-23MLD

Key Publishing – Pete West

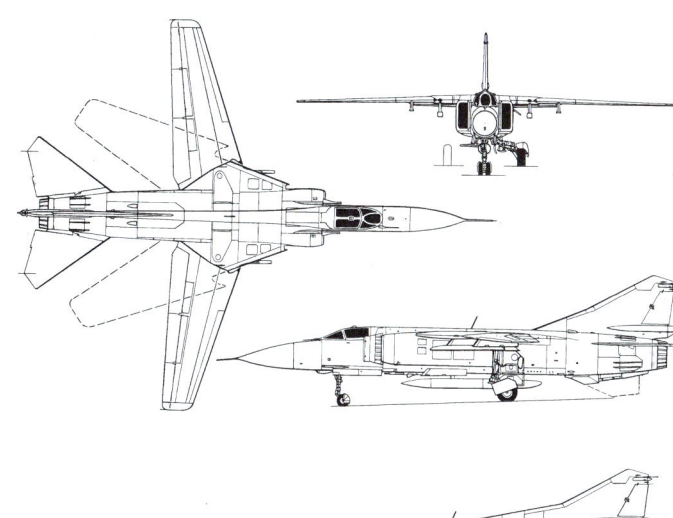

Crew	1
Length	51ft 4in (15.65m)
Wingspan (spread)	45ft 10in (13.97m)
Wingspan (swept)	25ft 6in (7.78m)
Height	15ft 10in (4.82m)
Wing Area (spread)	402ft² (37.35m²)
Wing Area (swept)	367ft² (34.16m²)
Empty Weight	21,153lbs (9,595kg)
Loaded Weight	32,400lbs (14,700kg)
Max Speed (Sea Level)	Mach 0.89 684mph/1,100km/h
Max Speed (at 42,000ft)	Mach 1.52 (1,168mph/1,880km/h)
Service Ceiling	60,695ft (18,500m)
Combat Range	710 miles (1,150km)

Powerplant: One 18,850lb/thrust (28,700lb/thrust in afterburner) Khatchaturov R-35-300 afterburning turbojet

Armament
One GSh-23L cannon plus two fuselage, two wing glove and two wing pylons with a capacity of up to 6,600lbs (3,000kg) of stores including S-5 rockets, up to 1,100lbs (500kg) of bombs and air-to-air and air-to-ground missiles including the R-60, R-73, R-23, R-77, R-27R and Kh-23 Grom.

ACTIVE DUTY

MiG-27 combat service with the Soviet Air Force was very limited. The Su-17 was employed extensively in Soviet-Afghan War but the MiG-27 was finally deployed to the region in 1988, with a single air regiment stocked with 36 MiG-27Ms and four MiG-23UB two-seaters arriving at Shinand AB. Even then the type was mostly used for high-altitude bombing attacks (instead of the ground attack role it was optimised for) and the aircraft saw little service before the withdrawal of Soviet forces in early 1989.

Although the MiG-23BN was exported widely the MiG-27 was only sold to India, Sri Lanka and Kazakhstan. Sri Lankan MiG-27s entered service in 2000 and have been used during the Sri Lankan Civil War to bomb ground targets and provide close air support.

Indian MiG-27s saw extensive combat, especially during the 1999 Kargil War, when one was lost together with a MiG-21 while supporting an Indian ground offensive in the Kashmir region.

The Indian Air Force retired its last MiG-27 squadron in December 2019. By 2021 only three were thought to be still in service with the Kazakh Air and Air Defence Forces whereas Russian and Ukrainian examples have long since retired.

For those air arms that retain their MiG-23 and MiG-27, the big variable-geometry winged jets remain a potent and reliable aircraft. Had the West met them over the German Plains they would have represented a considerable threat. ❖

By 2021 only three were thought to be still in service with the Kazakh Air and Air Defence Forces

MiG'S Fantastic *Fulcrum*

The MiG-29 is one of the most capable fighters the world has ever seen. Paul Fiddian and Steve Bridgewater turn their attention towards the past, present and future of the *Fulcrum*

Poland received its first batch of 12 *Fulcrums* (nine MiG-29As, three MiG-29UB) in 1989 and in 1995 ten used examples were acquired from the Czech Republic. A further 22 were received from the German Air Force in 2004 and 14 of these were overhauled and taken into service.
Rich Cooper/COAP Media

By the late 1960s aircraft manufacturers across the globe were giving thought to the next generation of fighter aircraft. In the USA, the Fighter Experimental (FX) programme was won by McDonnell Douglas in 1969 and its design would go on to become the highly successful F-15 Eagle.

This move prompted the USSR to issue a requirement for a similar heavy fighter to join the VVS. Designated the Prospective Frontal Fighter (Perspektivnyi Frontovoi Istrebitel/PFI), the requirement was actually fairly vague, but very ambitious. The new fighter needed high performance combined with excellent agility, long range and the ability to carry the latest and most sophisticated armament. At the same time it had to have the ability to operate from short, rough airstrips.

The competition was opened up to the Mikoyan and Sukhoi design bureaus and both companies set about creating PFI concepts, using recommendations from the Central Aerodynamics & Hydrodynamics Institute (Tsental'ny AeroGidrodinamicheski Institut/TsAGI) in Moscow.

It was Artem Mikoyan who realised that the ambitious requirements were impossible to meet with a single airframe so, in 1970, he lobbied the State to run two concurrent programmes: the Heavy PFI (Tyazholyi PFI/TPFI) and the Lightweight PFI (Logiky PFI/LPFI).

It was to be his last major victory at the helm of the company he co-created. Later in the year he would retire after a heart attack and on December 9, 1970 he passed away. His place was taken by Rostislav Belyakov, and under his direction the MiG OKB proceeded with both the TPFI and LPFI designs in memory of Mikoyan.

Interestingly, the USAF also went down the route of developing both heavyweight (and lightweight) fighters in the form of the F-15 Eagle and F-16 Fighting Falcon.

By the end of the contest the Sukhoi OKB was judged to have the best aircraft to meet the TPFI requirement whereas MiG was deemed to have the better LPFI design.

Left: The first prototype MiG-29 took to the skies for the first time on October 6, 1977. **Right:** The Klimov RD-33 turbofans were widely spaced and the area between them was used to create aerodynamic lift, thereby reducing the wing loading and improving manoeuvrability. In order to allow the aircraft to operate from very rough airstrips the main air inlet could be closed completely and air fed from auxiliary louvres on the upper fuselage for take-off, landing and low-altitude flying without the fear of ingesting debris. These louvres are evident in this image of a Soviet MiG-29A

FLANKER VS FULCRUM

Sukhoi's design would go on to become the highly successful Su-27 *Flanker* and the MiG lightweight fighter design would go on to become the MiG-29, which in turn would replace the MiG-21, MiG-23, Su-7, and Su-17 fighters in the VVS' Frontal (Tactical) Aviation section.

As the aircraft were both designed to meet the original PFI requirements, the MiG-and Su-27 shared broad aerodynamic similarities.

The MiG-29 had a mid-mounted swept-wing with blended leading-edge root extensions (LERXs). At the rear, the fighter had a highly swept tailplane and twin vertical fins; the latter mounted on booms outboard of the two engines.

The powerplants were Klimov RD-33 turbofans that could produce 18,277lb/thrust in full afterburner. The engines were widely spaced and the area between them was used to create aerodynamic lift, thereby reducing the wing loading and improving manoeuvrability.

Two large air intakes were located under the LERXs and were fitted with variable ramps to slow down the air at high-Mach speeds. In order to allow the aircraft to operate from very rough airstrips, the main air inlet could be closed completely and air fed from auxiliary louvres on the upper fuselage for take-off, landing and low-altitude flying without the fear of ingesting debris. The aircraft was also fitted with sturdy landing gear to enable it to use unprepared runways and the nosewheel could also be fitted with a mudguard.

Unlike the Su-27 the MiG design did not feature fly-by-wire controls but was naturally very agile. Tests proved it had an impressive instantaneous and sustained turn performance, could maintain very nose high (high alpha) attitudes and was very difficult to spin. The mostly aluminium airframe was stressed to +9G and was fitted with limiters that prevented the pilot from exceeding G and alpha limits – although they could be disabled manually.

The cockpit was also far simpler than its contemporaries' and had conventional 'non-glass' instrumentation with a head-up display and helmet mounted display, but no HOTAS (Hands On Throttle-And-Stick) capability. A Phazotron RLPK-29 radar fire control system with a N019 Sapfir 29 look-down/shoot-down pulse-Doppler radar and a Ts100.02-02 digital computer was also fitted – enabling the MiG-29 to track an enemy fighter at a range of 43 miles (70km).

Armament included a single 30mm GSh-30-1 cannon in the port wing root and three pylons were fitted below each wing. The inner pylons could accommodate fuel tanks, Vympel R-27 medium-range air-to-air missiles, unguided bombs or rockets whereas the outer pylons could carry R-73 or R-60 missiles. A single 330Imp Gal (1,500lit) fuel tank could also be fitted to the centreline, between the engines.

SPYING SATELLITE

Design work on the resultant Mikoyan Product 9 (later to be designated as the MiG-29A) began in 1974 under the leadership of Mikhail Waldenberg. By late 1975 progress was deemed so successful that the VVS issued a preliminary production contract at the same time it approved the production of development prototypes – the latter dubbed the Type 9-11.

The first prototype – aircraft '901' – was shipped to Zhukosvksy in mid 1977 for assembly and ground testing and on October 6 it performed the MiG-29's maiden flight. MiG OKB chief test pilot Alexander Fedotov was at the controls and he reported excellent handling.

The following month an overflying US spy satellite spotted the prototype at Zhukovsky; it was the first the West knew of the aircraft. After much deliberation NATO decided to give the aircraft the reporting name *Fulcrum*.

Test-flying continued apace with aircraft '902' and '904' joining the programme as development prototypes. These differed from '901' in that they had shorter nose gear and other changes. Aircraft '903' was lost when an engine caught fire mid-flight on June 15, 1978. Pilot Valeriy Menitskiy, ejected safely and MiG OKB provided aircraft '908' as a replacement. However, this aircraft was also lost in similar circumstances on October 31, 1980. Once again the pilot (this time Alexander Fedotov) ejected safely.

Nine pre-production prototypes (917 to 925) followed the development prototypes with the final example – which was essentially the same as the production Type 9-12 variant – taking to the skies for the first time in December 1982. The design was fundamentally the same as the original 9-11 concept, but by now the aircraft had a longer nose, taller tailfins, and a simplified canopy.

INTO SERVICE

The first examples joined VVS service in 1982 and proved very popular with their crews. The aircraft were simple to maintain and a joy to fly, although their relatively low fuel capacity relegated them to short-range air defence missions.

The MiG OKB initially built the basic Fulcrum in two main variants: the MiG-29A (9-12A) for use by the VVS and its Warsaw Pact allies and the MiG-29B (9-12B) for export to other nations. The latter had highly stripped-down avionics and lesser capabilities.

Although the *Fulcrum* was a relatively easy aircraft to fly there was demand for a two-seat operational conversion trainer version, especially from export customers. The first example flew on April 21, 1981 and was designated as the MiG-29UB (9-51).

Photographed in 1986 this is one of the VVS' first MiG-29 *Fulcrum-A* airframes.

The two-seater MiG-29UB featured a second cockpit that was only partially raised, in an attempt not to degrade the performance. As a result, the instructor in the rear had a generally poor view and a periscope automatically deployed when the undercarriage was lowered for landing.

The two-seater MiG-29's second cockpit was only partially raised, in an attempt not to degrade the performance. As a result, the instructor in the rear had a generally poor view and a periscope automatically deployed when the undercarriage was lowered for landing.

Since the MiG-29UB was not intended to be combat-capable, the radar was replaced by an on-board simulator module. The aircraft retained its 30mm cannon and could launch heat-seeking missiles, but not radar-guided missiles.

The type's UB suffix was deliberately misleading, since it stood for 'Uchebno-Boevoi' (Trainer-Combat) when the aircraft was really just a conversion trainer. NATO accepted the misinformation as it was provided and gave the variant the reporting name *Fulcrum-B*. (In reality it should have been given an 'M'-series name – as had the MiG-15UTI *Midget* and MiG-21UB *Mongol*).

Although US intelligence brought the MiG-29 to light within weeks of its first flight, a veil of secrecy had hung over it for many years. This became considerably more translucent when, on July 1, 1986, six MiG-29s in the service of the 234th Gvardeiskii Istrebitelnii Aviatsionnii Polk (234th Guards Fighter Aviation Regiment) at Kubinka AB, deployed to Kuopia Rissola, Finland. Soviet/Russian squadron exchanges were a regular occurrence but never before had the new fighter been involved.

As if to underline this changing of the guard, a solitary MiG-21 from the Finnish HavLv 31 squadron accompanied the sextet as it arrived, in delta formation, above the air base.

Display presentations formed part of the deployment, with both a solo and four-ship formation flown. This gave a taste of the MiG-29's performance capabilities but, still, much information was held back. Close-up ground inspections were available only to Finnish Air Force personnel and attending media representatives were given no structural, technical or operational data. Not too far into the future, all this would change.

FARNBOROUGH '88

News of two MiG-29s' participation in the 1988 Farnborough International Airshow emerged in June of that year. Today, it might have broken the internet – 30 years ago, it caused a major stir.

"If the two Soviet front-line fighters do appear at the show', wrote *Flight International*, in its June 11, 1988 edition, "it will be a major coup for the organiser, the Society of British Aerospace Companies (SBAC)."

Beyond 'unofficial' encounters, this would be the type's unveiling before Western eyes. "Their participation', *Flight* added, "in a major international air show such as Farnborough may be a genuine attempt to win more orders, or simply an exercise in aeronautical Glasnost."

The USSR certainly had plans to export the fighter en masse and by then the *Fulcrum* had already been sold to India, Iraq, North Korea, Syria and Yugoslavia. The presence of Waldenberg at Farnborough, probably related to this.

History was made when, mid-afternoon on August 30, the MiGs swept into view over Farnborough. Accompanying the two Fulcrums (which had flown in from Moscow, via a fuel stop at Wittstock, East Germany) was a pair of 5 Sqn Tornado F3s; the RAF jets having escorted the 'visitors' through UK airspace.

As they arrived overhead the airfield the Tornados peeled away allowing the two MiGs to carry out a brief but incendiary formation display beneath the dark clouds. Its conclusion was a pairs landing on Runway 25 against the symbolic backdrop of Farnborough's iconic black sheds and the Antonov An-124 *Ruslan* strategic airlifter that had already arrived. Wheel contact; the 'pop' of their braking parachutes and deceleration – all took place in near-perfect synchronisation. The Soviets were clearly out to impress but this was just the beginning.

The Russians had brought a single-seat MiG-29A and a two-seat MiG-29UB and from the cockpits, test pilots Anatoly Kvotchur and Roman Taskaev climbed down before a fascinated crowd of reporters and broadcasters.

Media interest was, naturally, extremely high and exceptionally far-reaching. That the MiGs were even here was a revelation – that both pilots would subsequently demonstrate the single-seater so impressively came as a lightning bolt to the West.

Limited to four minutes' duration by the SBAC – the standard Farnborough solo display length of the day – the MiG-29's blazing routines were the

History is made as the first two MiG-29s to visit the West land at Farnborough on August 30, 1988.

The Russian MiG-29 crews pose with their Tornado 'escorts' after landing at Farnborough.

Anatoly Kvotchur blasts into the Farnborough sky in the MiG-29 in 1988 at the start of one of his legendary displays.

Left: In July 1993, two MiG-29s of the Russian Air Force Test Pilots team collided in mid-air at the International Air Tattoo at RAF Fairford. No one on the ground sustained any serious injuries, and the two pilots ejected and landed safely. **Right:** A number of display teams have operated the MiG-29, most notably the Russian Air Force Swifts. *MiGAvia/Russian Aircraft Corporation*

undisputed highlight of Farnborough '88. Both Kvotchur and Taskaev flew during the week but it's the former's displays that, partly through the extent of press coverage, are best-remembered now.

A dramatically short take-off run preceded an opening loop, this an effective power-to-weight ratio showcase in its own right. Then came the tail-slide. Jaws dropped, eyes were rubbed and pre-conceptions were reset each time. The manoeuvre brought about a seismic shift in airshow performance terms: such behaviour almost being expected of MiG-29 displays thereafter. As Kvotchur and others would repeatedly stress, however, this wasn't just a party trick but, rather, a capability with genuine frontline combat relevance. Dropping through its RD-33s' pluming smoke carpet, the aircraft swung round into a 'high-alpha' pass before powering up into a quarter-clover loop. Next was a knife-edge pass, sustained along the length of the display line that underlined the abundance of lift supplied by the fuselage, nacelles and fins. The final figures were a half-Cuban, a wrenching 9G turn, afterburners glowing, and a Derry turn into landing.

On September 12, after a two-week stay, the MiG-29s left Farnborough as they'd arrived, in formation. This time, though, it was a pair of Sea Harrier FRS1s that joined them, the quartet undertaking a low-level beat up in a farewell salute.

Those displays of 1988 established a tradition of jaw-dropping MiG-29 routines at British airshows that continue to this day.

By the mid-1980s, a new version of the original MiG-29 was proposed to meet the Soviet western frontline requirement. Provisionally named the MiG-33 it needed to be a multirole fighter and ground attack airframe and also feature a considerably increased combat range. The new aircraft was eventually developed as the MiG-29M *Fulcrum-E* variant a two-seat model (the MiG-29MRCA) was MiG's contender for various international fighter aircraft bids and the type has been constantly upgraded over the years.

MiG-29M

By the mid-1980s, a new version of the original MiG-29 was proposed to meet the Soviet western frontline requirement. Provisionally named the MiG-33, it needed to be a multi-role fighter and ground attack airframe and also feature a considerably increased combat range.

The new aircraft was eventually developed as the MiG-29M *Fulcrum-E* variant and benefited from a redesigned airframe constructed from a lightweight aluminium-lithium alloy to increase the thrust-to-weight ratio. The upper intake louvres were removed to make way for more fuel in the LERXs and mesh screens introduced to prevent foreign object damage to the engine.

A two-seat model (the MiG-29MRCA) was MiG's contender for various international fighter aircraft bids and the type has been constantly upgraded over the years.

UPGRADES

Even as the *Fulcrum A* was being introduced into production, the MiG OKB was giving thought to an upgraded version. Dubbed the Type 9-13 or MiG-29S, the new variant housed a Gardeniya active jammer module in a swollen spine that resulted in Soviet pilots nicknaming it 'Gorbatyi' (Hunchback). It looked so different from the earlier version that NATO dubbed it the *Fulcrum-C*. ➡

Left: East Germany bought 24 MiG-29s (including four MiG-29UBs), which entered service in 1988–1989. After the reunification of Germany in 1990, the MiG-29s and other aircraft of the East German Air Forces of the National People's Army were integrated into the West German Luftwaffe. **Right:** The only New World nations to obtain the MiG-29 for operational service were Cuba and Peru – the latter acquired 21 MiG-29S fighters from Belarus in 1997 and three more from Russia a year later. Peru later paid Mikoyan to upgrade eight aircraft to MiG-29SMP standard. *MiGAvia/Russian Aircraft Corporation*

Yugoslav *Fulcrums* were involved in the Kosovo War and although the jets saw little in the way of combat six were shot down during the NATO intervention in the war.

The Indian MiG-29UPG is similar to the SMT variant but differs by having a foreign-made avionics suite. The type performed its maiden flight on February 4, 2011. *MiGAvia/Russian Aircraft Corporation*

Around 200 *Fulcrum-Cs* were built, with the first entering squadron service in 1986. The variant was not initially exported as the USSR did not want to share the countermeasure technology. However, a MiG-29SE variant, with downgraded performance was later offered to friendly air arms. The jets' inner underwing pylons could carry over 1,102lbs (500kg) as well as R-27T1, R-27ER1 and R-27ET1 medium-range missiles.

The original *Fulcrum* airframe proved to be very adaptable and MiG was able to produce a number of spin-off variants. The MiG-29SM (Type 9.13M) was similar to the basic *Fulcrum-C* but could carry guided air-to-surface missiles and TV- and laser-guided bombs.

The MiG-29SM (SyAF) was developed for the Syrian Air Force and used the Type 9.12 airframe but had similar capabilities to the MiG-29SM.

East Germany flew the MiG-29G and MiG-29GT variant – these being single and two-seat versions upgraded to meet NATO avionics and radio standards. Meanwhile, the Slovak Air Force operated the MiG-29AS/MiG-29UBS, which were variants of the MiG-29S that had also been upgraded for NATO compatibility.

The MiG OKB and a series of Israeli firms also collaborated on the MiG-29 Sniper programme to upgrade early Romanian Air Force MiG-29 airframes. The first example flew in May 2000 but the project was cancelled in 2003 when Romania retired its *Fulcrum* fleet due to excessive maintenance costs. The nation upgraded its MiG-21s instead.

Other upgrades included the MiG-29SMT (Type 9.17), which modified first-generation MiG-29s to MiG-29M configuration complete with additional fuel tanks in an enlarged spine. The cockpit also had an enhanced HOTAS design and glass screen technology.

The Indian MiG-29UPG version is similar to the SMT but differs by having a foreign-made avionics suite integrated within it. The type performed its maiden flight on February 4, 2011.

Two of the eight MiG-29s currently in service with the Bangladesh Air Force. *Bangladesh Air Force*

The Russian Navy ordered 24 MiG-29Ks in late 2009 for use aboard the *Admiral Kuznetsov*. Deliveries began in 2010 and in October 2016 four aircraft from the 100th Independent Shipborne Fighter Aviation Regiment formed part of the air group aboard the carrier as it deployed to the Mediterranean Sea as part of the Russian campaign in Syria. *MiGAvia/Russian Aircraft Corporation*

MiG and a series of Israeli firms also collaborated on the MiG-29 Sniper programme to upgrade early Romanian Air Force MiG-29 airframes. The first example flew in May 2000 but the project was cancelled in 2003 when Romania retired its *Fulcrum* fleet due to excessive maintenance costs.

EXPORT OPERATORS

As with so many MiG designs the *Fulcrum* was exported widely to friendly Eastern Bloc nations such as Bulgaria, Czechoslovakia, East Germany, Hungary, Poland, Romania, and Yugoslavia.

Following the collapse of the USSR large numbers of VVS MiG-29s were passed onto newly formed independent states including Belarus, Kazakhstan, Moldova, Turkmenistan, Ukraine, and Uzbekistan. Serbia inherited the ex-Yugoslavian MiGs following the nation's civil war.

The Fulcrum was also exported on a large scale to nations around the globe. In Africa it served with the air arms of Algeria, Eritrea, and Sudan and in the Middle East it flew with the air forces of Iraq, Iran, Syria and Yemen.

The type also proved popular in Asia with Bangladesh, Malaysia and North Korea flying different versions of the type. India was the first international customer of the MiG-29 when the Indian Air Force placed an order for more than 50 airframes in 1980.

The only New World nations to obtain the MiG-29 for operational service were Cuba and Peru but the USA acquired at least 20 examples from Moldova for evaluation and use in adversary training.

COMBAT EXPERIENCE

MiG-29s of various air arms have seen combat over the past few decades.

Yugoslav *Fulcrums* were involved in the Kosovo War, but the jets saw little in the way of combat. In 1991, several Croatian Antonov An-2 aircraft were destroyed on the ground at Čepin airfield near Osijek, Croatia by a Yugoslav MiG-29 and later in the year two MiG-29s carried out an airstrike on Banski dvori, the official residence of the Croatian Government.

A total of six MiG-29s were shot down during the NATO intervention in the war; three falling to the guns of USAF F-15s, one to a USAF F-16 and one to a Royal Netherlands Air Force F-16. The sixth example was hit by friendly fire from the ground and another four MiG-29s were destroyed on the ground.

Iraqi MiG-29s were involved in the later stages of the Iran–Iraq War with at least one example downed by an Iranian F-14 Tomcat. Iraqi *Fulcrums* were also involved in the 1991 Gulf War with five being shot down by USAF F-15s. The nation's fleet of 37 MiG-29s was reduced to just 12 examples by the end of the Gulf War; all of which were retired in 1995.

In 1996 a Cuban MiG-29UB allegedly shot down two Cessna 337s belonging to the organisation Brothers to the Rescue, after the aircraft approached Cuban airspace.

Indian Air Force MiG-29s were used extensively during the 1999 Kargil War in Kashmir and flown as fighter escorts for Mirage 2000s. According to some Indian sources, two MiG-29s gained missile lock on Pakistani F-16s but did not engage them because no official declaration of war had been issued.

During the 1999 Eritrean-Ethiopian War, a number of Eritrean MiG-29s were shot down by Ethiopian Su-27s piloted by Russian mercenaries and there are claims that Eritrean MiG-29s shot down two Ethiopian MiG-21s, three MiG-23s, and an Su-25.

Syrian Air Force *Fulcrums* have regularly encountered Israeli aircraft and in 1989 a pair of Israeli F-15Cs reportedly shot down two Syrian MiG-29s. It is claimed Israeli F-15s shot down two Syrian *Fulcrums* off the coast of Lebanon in September 2001 but both Syria and Israel deny the claim. In more recent years Syrian MiG-29s entered the nation's civil war in October 2013, attacking Free Syrian Army insurgents with unguided rockets and bombs.

During the 2008 Darfur War in Sudan one of the nation's MiG-29s was downed by ground fire from rebel group the Justice and Equality Movement. The aircraft was allegedly piloted by a Russian mercenary, who was killed.

On April 20, 2008, a Russian MiG-29 shot down a Georgian Hermes 450 UAV (unmanned aerial vehicle) with a R-73 heat-seeking missile – although Russia denies the claim. Likewise, it denies the shooting down of a Ukrainian Sukhoi Su-25 *Frogfoot* by a MiG-29 in Ukraine on July 16, 2014. During the Russian 'military intervention' in Crimea in 2014, Russian forces also allegedly captured up to 45 Ukrainian Air Force MiG-29s at Belbek AB.

Iran is thought to still have in excess of 20 MiG-29s. They operate alongside the remnants of the nation's F-14 Tomcat fleet.

The MiG-29 replaced the MiG-21 in various air arms – including the Czech Air Force.

Left: In typically Russian style the MiG-29 was built to take a significant amount of 'punishment'. This example is dragging its jet pipes along the runway as the pilot keeps the nose high for aerodynamic braking. **Right:** The RD-33 turbofans were notoriously smoky so later upgrades have focuses on engine technology to reduce the type's carbon output.

Upgrades have included the MiG-29SMT, which modified first-generation MiG-29s to MiG-29M configuration complete with additional fuel tanks in an enlarged spine. The cockpit also had an enhanced HOTAS design and glass screen technology. *MiGAvia/Russian Aircraft Corporation*

Undeniably the most dramatic performer of all *Fulcrums*, the MiG-29OVT serves as a testbed for thrust vectoring engine and fly-by-wire technology. Based upon the MiG-29M the aircraft features RD-133 engines with unusual 3D thrust-vectoring nozzles. *MiGAvia/Russian Aircraft Corporation*

The MiG-29SMT became a regular fixture at airshows across the world as Mikoyan tried to sell it to air arms around the globe. *MiGAvia/Russian Aircraft Corporation*

Left: Among the more stylish markings applied to the *Fulcrum* was this Slovakian MiG-29UBS. *MiGAvia/Russian Aircraft Corporation* **Right:** Now referred to as the MiG-35 and designated *Fulcrum-F* by NATO the latest variant of the type was unveiled in 2007 by Russian Minister of Defence, Sergey Ivanov when visited the Lukhovitsky Machine Building Plant in early 2007. *MiGAvia/Russian Aircraft Corporation*

The MiG-35 is classed as a 4++ generation fighter and forms the basis of the current Mikoyan sales drive *MiGAvia/Russian Aircraft Corporation*

In 2014, Egypt signed a deal with Russia for the purchase of 24 MiG-35s and this was increased to 46 aircraft a year later. The first batch was transferred to Egypt in April 2017. *MiGAvia/Russian Aircraft Corporation*

Other Ukrainian *Fulcrums* were involved in the military operation, performing combat air patrols and show of force flights and on August 7 a Ukrainian Air Force MiG-29MU1 was shot down by an anti-aircraft missile fired by pro-Russian rebels near Yenakievo. Ten days later another *Fulcrum* was shot down by pro-Russian rebels in the Luhansk region.

In total, since it was introduced to service the MiG-29 has scored an estimated six air-to-air victories but at the loss of around 18 jets in air-to-air combat or to ground fire.

NEXT GENERATION *FULCRUMS*

Over the years MiG OKB continued to tweak the basic *Fulcrum* design with the addition of lithium-aluminium alloy and composite components to reduce weight, simplify manufacture, and increase the useful internal volume of the aircraft.

Modernised cockpit systems were also introduced to reduce pilot workload and the avionics were continually upgraded.

Perhaps the most radical modification to the airframe came about with the MiG-29K (Type 9.31) naval variant. The carrier-based *Fulcrum* had a much stronger undercarriage, an arrestor hook, corrosion proofing and new hydraulically-folding wings. The wings featured a double slotted flap system to improve low-speed handling and power came from navalised RD-33K engines with improved spool up times to help in the event of a balked landing.

SPECIFICATION MIKOYAN-GUREVICH MIG-29 *FULCRUM-A*

Key Publishing – Pete West

Crew	1
Length	56ft 10in (17.32m)
Wingspan	37ft 3in (11.36m)
Height	15ft 6in (4.73m)
Wing Area	409ft² (38.00m²)
Empty Weight	24,250lbs (11,000kg)
Loaded Weight	33,730lbs (14,900kg)
Max Speed	(Sea Level) Mach 1.21 930mph/1,500km/h
Max Speed	at 42,000ft) Mach 2.25 (1,490mph/2,400km/h)
Service Ceiling	59,100ft (18,000m)
Combat Range	888 miles (1,430km)
Powerplant:	Two 18,342lb/thrust Klimov RD-33 afterburning turbofans

Armament
One GSh-301 autocannon plus seven pylons with a capacity of 8,800lbs (4,000kg) of freefall bombs, rockets and air-to-air missiles including the R-27 (x4), R-60 (x4) and R-73 (x2).

Originally intended for the *Admiral Kuznetsov class* aircraft carriers, the first flight of MiG-29K prototype was on June 23, 1988 but the collapse of the USSR meant the type was not put into production for many years.

The MiG Corporation restarted the programme in 1999 and in 2004 the Indian Navy signed a contract for 12 single-seat MiG-29K and four two-seat MiG-29KUB variants. The new MiG-29K has radar absorbing coatings to reduce its radar signature signature and is referred to by NATO as the *Fulcrum-D*.

Undeniably the most dramatic performer of all *Fulcrums*, the MiG-29OVT serves as a testbed for thrust vectoring engine and fly-by-wire technology. Based upon the MiG-29M the aircraft features RD-133 engines with unusual 3D thrust-vectoring nozzles.

Four decades after its maiden flight the sun has far from set on the career of MiG's legendary *Fulcrum*. *Rich Cooper/COAP Media*

MIG-35 – 21ST CENTURY *FULCRUM*

Thirty years after the first MiG-29 flew, Mikoyan-Gurevich debuted the latest version of the *Fulcrum* in 2007.

Now referred to as the MiG-35 and designated *Fulcrum-F* by NATO, the new aircraft is a multi-role fighter that was developed from the MiG-29M/M2 and MiG-29K/KUB series of aircraft.

Classed as a 4+ generation fighter, the first of ten prototypes was actually a modified MiG-29M2 model demonstrator. The aircraft was unveiled in 2007 by Russian Minister of Defence, Sergey Ivanov when he visited the Lukhovitsky Machine Building Plant in early 2007 and the aircraft debuted at that year's Aero India airshow in Bangalore.

India was chosen for the debut because the MiG-35 was to be a contender with the Eurofighter Typhoon, Boeing F/A-18E/F Super Hornet, Dassault Rafale, Saab JAS 39 Gripen and General Dynamics F-16 Fighting Falcon in the competition to provide the Indian Air Force with 126 multi-role combat aircraft.

Compared to the MiG-29M from which it was developed, the MiG-35's most notable changes include the addition of a Phazotron Zhuk AE active electronically scanned array (AESA) radar and a newly designed OLS-35 optical locator system. The number of weapon pylons also increased to ten while the aircraft has been made more stealthy and the range increased by more than 50%. Mikoyan-Gurevich also claims that the operating costs have decreased by a factor of 2.5 compared to earlier MiG-29s.

The MiG-35 is fitted the latest version of the RD-33 engines (the 19,841lb/thrust RD-33MK). These produce 7% more power thanks to the use of modern materials in the cooled blades. They are also 'smokeless' and can be fitted with vectored-thrust nozzles if required.

According to Mikoyan the MiG-35 had a unit cost of around US$45 million and in January 2017 the type was demonstrated to the Russian government and interested export nations. The first two serial production aircraft were delivered to the Russian Aerospace Forces on June 17, 2019. Russia is the only current customer.

As the *Fulcrum* enters its fourth decade the MiG-35 and countless MiG-29 upgrade options provided by the modern-day Mikoyan and Russian Aircraft Corporation seem set to ensure the charismatic fighter will be a familiar sight in the skies for decades to come. ❖

Foxbat out of Hell

A total of 1,186 MiG-25s were built by Mikoyan-Gurevich between 1964 and 1984

In 1976 an audacious Russian pilot defected to Japan in a Soviet MiG-25 *Foxbat*. Steven Taylor tells the story of this incredible event in Cold War history, which caused consternation in Moscow and a sensation in the West

The mighty fighter jet sat 200ft beyond the main runway, where it had slewed to a halt just moments earlier. It was a unique visitor to the civil airport at Hakodate, on the southern tip of the Japanese home island of Hokkaido, and its dramatic, unannounced arrival that Monday afternoon in September 1976 quickly drew a crowd of curious and bemused onlookers.

Some of the more aeronautically-minded among them may have recognised the distinctive boxy, muscular shape of the aircraft. All, however, would surely have immediately identified the red star insignia of the Soviet Air Force adorning the plane's tail fins.

What the crowd of travellers and airport staff were witnessing unfold that September day 47 years ago was one of the most extraordinary episodes of the Cold War: the defection by a Russian pilot in the Soviet Union's most advanced and formidable warplane, the legendary Mikoyan-Gurevich MiG-25 *Foxbat*.

At the time, the MiG-25 was the fastest, highest flying interceptor in the world, its nickel alloy and titanium construction, and two huge Tumansky R-15 turbojet engines allowing it to travel at a top speed of 1,886kts and up to an altitude of 85,000ft. The only aircraft that could fly higher and faster was the SR-71 Blackbird spy plane.

The MiG made its international public debut at the Domodedovo Airshow on July 9, 1967, and NATO assigned the new fighter the reporting name *Foxbat*.

In 1971 a detachment of MiG-25s was deployed to Egypt, where their Soviet pilots conducted photo-reconnaissance sorties over the Israeli-occupied Sinai Peninsula on behalf of Egypt's President Sadat. Despite the best efforts of Israeli F-4 Phantom II pilots to shoot them down, including one attempt on November 6, 1971 using specially lightened Phantoms, the *Foxbats* proved immune to interception.

But it was as an air defence interceptor that the *Foxbat* really had NATO worried, and the Americans, in particular, were desperate to get their hands on an example. Fortunately, one was about to land in their lap, courtesy of a disillusioned Soviet pilot.

◀ Belenko's Foxbat passes the runway lights at Hakodate at high speed. This photo was taken on the evening of September 6, 1976 as the Soviet pilot was 'delivering' the West its first MiG-25

 ▶ Former Soviet pilot Viktor Belenko's military identity document; as carried on his famous flight to Japan
(CIA Archives)

▲ The MiG-25 *Foxbat* features a powerful radar and four air-to-air missiles and has an operational top speed of Mach 2.83 - although Mach 3.2 is possible this risks significant damage to the engines USAF Museum

◄ When first seen in reconnaissance photography, the *Foxbat's* large wing suggested a highly manoeuvrable fighter. The capabilities of the MiG-25 were only understood in 1976 when Belenko defected to Japan and it turned out that it was the aircraft's weight that necessitated its large wings USAF Museum

DESPERATE DEFECTOR

Victor Ivanovich Belenko was born in the city of Nalchik in the northern Caucasus in 1947, the son of a miner and veteran of the Great Patriotic War. After first enrolling in medical school, he changed career direction two years later, his love of aviation leading him into the Soviet Air Force Military Academy in Armavir, in the province of Krasnodar Krai. After graduating he was assigned to a MiG-17 training squadron in 1970.

Both professionally and personally Belenko's life appeared settled. In 1973 he married Ludmilla and the couple had a son, Dmitri. The next year 1st Lieutenant Belenko gained a transfer to the elite 513th Fighter Regiment of the PVO (Soviet Air Defence Command), equipped with the Soviets' latest fighter, the MiG-25P, based at Chuguyevka in the Russian Far East.

But in reality all was not well. Belenko was secretly harbouring growing anti-communist feelings and becoming increasingly disillusioned with the Soviet regime, which he later described as a 'corrupt, abusive system'. His marriage was also on the rocks.

By the summer of 1976 he had decided to defect in his MiG-25. But it would be no easy task; the nearest non-communist state to his base was Japan, some 435 miles away, close to the limit of the MiG-25's range. And if the Soviets didn't shoot Belenko down after realising he was defecting, he risked being intercepted by the Japanese, who had a strong air defence system in place.

At 12.50pm on September 6, Belenko took off from Chuguyevka. Flying MiG-25P '31', which had only rolled off the production line at the Gorky aviation plant in February that year; he was part of a five-strong formation on a routine training flight. All were unarmed.

A few minutes into the sortie Belenko climbed to 19,000ft and then suddenly put the huge 32-ton fighter into a steep dive and disappeared into cloud, watched by his shocked squadron mates, who thought he had lost control of his aircraft.

Belenko's MiG disappeared from Soviet radar and neither the other pilots nor Chuguyevka control could raise him on the radio. By the time the rest of the squadron landed back at base it was assumed Belenko had crashed into the sea and tragically killed.

" The MiG-25 was the fastest, highest flying interceptor in the world "

In fact, once he had descended through the clouds and was out of visual contact, Belenko levelled off at 100ft, switched off his radar and radio, and set course for Hokkaido, intending to land at the Chitose military base. To avoid being picked up by Soviet radar, he remained below 200ft for most of the flight, even though the thirsty MiG would burn up fuel much more quickly at low altitude.

INTRUDER DETECTED

Two hundred miles off the coast of Hokkaido, over the Sea of Japan, the *Foxbat* – now flying at higher altitude since Belenko considered himself clear of Soviet defences – was picked up on Japanese radar. The Japanese attempted to raise the mystery aircraft on radio, ordering it to divert, and when they failed a pair of F-4 Phantom IIs of the Japanese Air Self Defence Force were rerouted to intercept. But the Phantoms were unable to reach the lightning quick Soviet interceptor.

After a flight lasting almost an hour, Belenko was approaching the Japanese mainland when a red warning light suddenly began flashing on his instrument panel. He didn't have enough fuel left to make it to Chitose, and so instead Belenko diverted to the nearer civil airport at Hakodate.

Abandoning his first landing attempt when he saw a Boeing 727 taking off, he circled the airport and came in for a second approach, this time touching down safely. But as the fighter thundered along the tarmac the Soviet pilot realised with mounting alarm that there wasn't enough runway in which to stop the big MiG-25. After deploying his braking parachutes, he juddered to a standstill 200ft beyond the end of the runway, bursting a tyre in the process.

As amazed spectators gingerly approached the exotic-looking aircraft, the Russian airman opened the canopy and, having no English or Japanese, fired two shots in the air from his service pistol to warn them away. After a nervy stand-off an airport official waving a white flag warily approached, to whom Belenko passed a scribbled note, which read: 'Quickly call representative American intelligence service'.

It was now clear to the Japanese that they were dealing not with an accidental landing by a pilot who'd simply lost his bearings but rather a defection. An interpreter was summoned from Sapporo and, after an initial interrogation during which the pilot requested political asylum in the US, he was flown by police helicopter first to Chitose, his original destination, and then onto Iruma AB near Tokyo by military transport for further questioning.

News of Belenko's flight to Japan in the MiG caused consternation in Moscow and a sensation in the West. The Soviet embassy demanded immediate access to the pilot, as did the Americans.

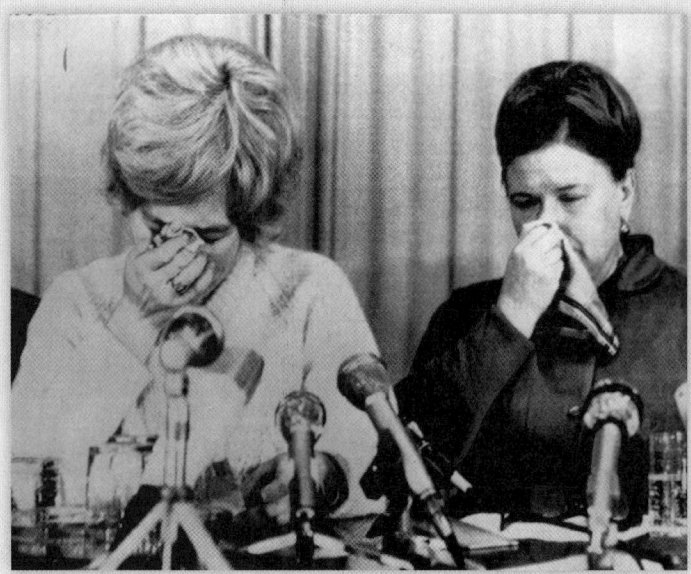
Lyudmila Petrovna Belenko, left, and Lyudmila Stepanova Belenko, wife and mother of Viktor Belenko, tell a Moscow press conference that his flight was not a defection.

With tarpaulins draped over the wing Japanese crews begin to recover the stricken MiG from the grass at the end of Hakodate's runway.

By the time this image was taken the tell-tale red stars had been removed from the aircraft. Belenko was not the first pilot to have defected from the Soviet-bloc in this way. In March and May 1953, two Polish Air Force pilots flew MiG-15s to Denmark and in 1953 North Korean pilot No Kum Sok flew his MiG-15 to an American base in South Korea. On May 20, 1989 Soviet Captain Aleksandr Zuyev flew his MiG-29 to Trabzon, Turkey on May 20.

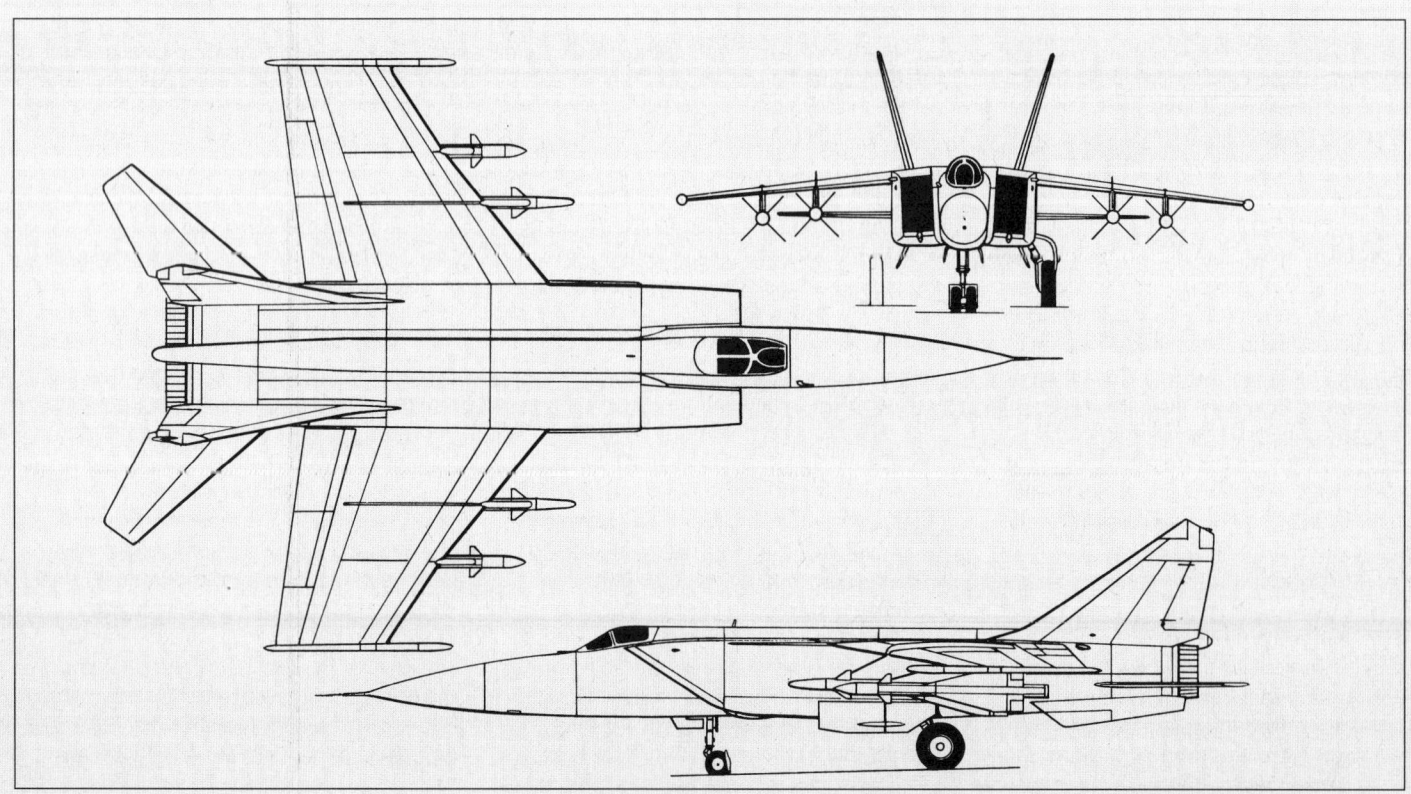

The MiG-25's two Tumansky R-15B-300 afterburning turbojets each produce 22,494lb/thrust in full reheat

The Japanese, unsure what to do, played for time, charging the Soviet airman with violating Japanese airspace and illegal possession of a firearm.

MAJOR COUP

Belenko's landing in Japan was, of course, a major embarrassment for Moscow, which quickly put out a story that that the pilot had become lost during a routine training flight, was forced to land in Japan owing to low fuel and was now being held against his will by the Japanese authorities.

Under pressure, the Japanese persuaded Belenko to meet with an official from the Soviet embassy. The seven-minute meeting between Belenko and the official – who was also the embassy's resident KGB officer – was a stormy one, the KGB man allegedly calling Belenko a 'traitor' when he rejected the embassy's offer to have him repatriated.

Belenko then met with the Americans and three days after his dramatic arrival on Hokkaido, he was flown to Langley Air Force base in Virginia.

At a time when they were still licking their wounds from Vietnam, the defection of Victor Belenko was a major propaganda coup for the Americans, and on September 13, 1976 President Gerald Ford held a press conference in which he personally confirmed that the Russian airman would be granted asylum. "This is a tradition in the United States," declared the President, "and as long as he wants such asylum, he will be granted it in the United States."

Moscow could no longer hide the truth that Belenko had voluntarily defected. In a statement issued through the state-

"Tokyo returned the dismantled fighter in 30 crates"

controlled TASS news agency the day after President Ford's announcement, the furious Soviet government lashed out at the Japanese: "The acts of [the] Japanese authorities with regard to the Soviet plane and its pilot could not be qualified as being other than unfriendly to the Soviet Union, flouting elementary norms of international law and the practices of relations between states, especially neighbour states."

Moscow then resorted to emotional blackmail, holding a press conference on September 28, in which Belenko's mother and wife Ludmilla pleaded with the rogue pilot to return to Russia. "I was officially reassured at the highest level here that you will be forgiven, even if you made a mistake," his wife Ludmilla assured him.

But Victor had no intention of returning to Russia. For the next five months he was extensively debriefed by the CIA at Langley, providing his hosts with a wealth of intelligence on the inner workings of the Soviet PVO, including insights into the morale of its personnel, which according to Belenko was "poor". He also revealed that the Soviets were developing a more advanced version of the *Foxbat* (this being the MiG-31, which entered service in 1981 and was given the codename *Foxhound* by NATO).

Meanwhile, the prized *Foxbat* was moved by USAF C-5 Galaxy to Hyakuri Air Base on September 25, 1976, where the Japanese permitted a technical team from the USAF's Foreign Technology Division, based at Wright-Patterson Air Force Base, to dismantle and examine the fighter in minute detail. "Frankly, this MiG-25 was way beyond us," a Japanese official admitted to the press. "We had to have help."

The MiG-25 made its international public debut at the Domodedovo Airshow on July 9, 1967.

A pair of F-4 Phantom IIs of the Japanese Air Self Defence Force were routed to intercept the MiG but failed to reach it in time. *USAF*

UNDERESTIMATED

However, in spite of the ease with which Belenko's *Foxbat* had penetrated Japan's air defences, the Americans were on the whole left rather unimpressed by the aircraft, and particularly by its avionics, judging it to be inferior in most respects to the latest generation of US fighters like the F-15 Eagle.

While the American experts were poring over every inch of the *Foxbat*, Moscow continued to press the Japanese for its return. Two months after Belenko's defection, with the US inspection complete, Tokyo finally relented, sending the dismantled fighter in 30 crates to the port of Hitachi, where it was collected by a Soviet freighter on November 15, and arrived in Vladivostok several days later.

"The return of the MiG-25 will remove a major irritant in Soviet-Japanese relations, and both countries seem anxious to put the problem behind them," a US National Intelligence cable observed that month.

But Moscow would not forgive Victor Belenko. He was sentenced to death for treason in absentia and, to discourage any other would-be defectors, the KGB spread a rumour that he had been killed in an unfortunate 'accident' in the US.

In fact, Victor Belenko was busy building a new life for himself in America. He became an aerospace engineering consultant and in 1980, the same year that he was granted US citizenship, co-

" I merely changed my flight plan slightly in the air "

authored his autobiography *MiG Pilot*, which detailed his defection. He also began a new family, marrying a music teacher from North Dakota, and the couple had two sons, though the marriage later broke down.

Belenko never had any regrets about his decision to defect. "I love this country," he said of his adopted homeland in a 2000 interview – and after the fall of the Soviet Union, he was able to visit Russia again in 1996. Belenko was not, however, impressed by what he found. "That country is still a closed society," he said at the time.

But while the *Foxbat* didn't win the Cold War for the Soviet Union, the US technical team which examined Belenko's MiG-25 in 1976 may have been a little hasty in dismissing it. Though Syrian examples fared poorly over Lebanon in the early 1980s, with several being shot down by the Israelis, Iraqi MiG-25s enjoyed considerable success in the Iran-Iraq War, destroying a number of Iranian aircraft.

And the Americans themselves suffered their only air-to-air combat loss of Operation *Desert Storm* at the hands of a MiG-25 pilot, an Iraqi *Foxbat* downing a US Navy F/A-18 Hornet on the opening night of the Gulf War (the Iraqi Air force's only aerial victory of the conflict).

As for Victor Belenko, the man who handed the West one of the greatest prizes of the Cold War, he always maintained that he didn't actually steal the *Foxbat*. Rather, the pilot insisted, he merely "changed my flight plan slightly in the air". ❖

Until Belenko landed in Japan this was as close as Westerners had got to a *Foxbat*. USAF

The first prototype MiG-25 was a reconnaissance variant, designated the Ye-155-R1. It made its maiden flight on March 6, 1964 and had some characteristics that were unique to that prototype. The wings had fixed wingtip tanks to which small winglets were attached for stability purposes, but when it was found that fuel sloshing around in the tanks caused vibrations they were eliminated from further models. The aircraft also had attachments for movable foreplanes, to help with pitch control at high speed. The subsequent Ye-155-R3 was made lighter by removing some unneeded equipment and used for record attempts. The first claim was for a world speed record with no payload and MiG OKB Chief Test Pilot Alexander V Fedotov reached an average speed of 1,441.07mph over a 1,000 km circuit on March 16, 1965. The aircraft later reached 1,852.67mph for a pure speed record.

"A Wanton Attack"
The RAF's first Cold War loss

That was how a furious Winston Churchill described the shooting down of an RAF Avro Lincoln bomber by Soviet MiG-15 jet fighters in March 1953. Now, 70 years on, mystery still surrounds the tragic final flight of Lincoln RF531. Steven Taylor investigates

Andy Hay/www.flyingart.co.uk

On March 12, 1953 the Cold War suddenly turned very hot for the RAF. For it was on this day that Soviet fighters finally brought down a British aircraft, in an uneven contest between an ageing Avro Lincoln and a MiG-15 jet.

The first months of 1953 were a particularly tense time in the history of the undeclared conflict between the Soviet Union and the West. The nuclear arms race was at its most intense, the Korean War was still raging and the death of Stalin in early March had plunged the Kremlin into a leadership crisis. Meanwhile, the air forces of the West, primarily – but not exclusively – the USAF and RAF, were regularly conducting clandestine 'spy flights' over Soviet territory, photographing sensitive military installations, testing response times of scrambled fighters and gathering electronic intelligence (ELINT), such as recording Russian radar emissions.

The Soviet Air Force reacted forcefully to these intrusions. In June 1952 a DC-3 of the Swedish Air Force, believed to be on a secret ELINT mission, was intercepted and shot down by a MiG fighter over the Baltic, with the loss of all eight crewmen. Then, on March 10, 1953 a USAF F-84 Thunderjet was also shot down, again by a MiG fighter, this time after apparently breaching Czech airspace.

Nor were these incidents confined to military aircraft. On April 29, 1952 an Air France C-54 en route to West Berlin was badly damaged by two MiG-15s, necessitating an emergency landing at Tempelhof airport. It was later found to have been struck by no fewer than 89 cannon shells, though miraculously none of the passengers or crew were seriously injured.

DIRE WARNING

It was against this backdrop of high tension in the skies over Central Europe that a 192 Sqn Avro Lincoln, attached to the Central Gunnery School at RAF Leconfield in Yorkshire, set out on what was later described by the British government as a "routine flight" to West Germany.

Piloted by 29-year-old Flight Sergeant Peter Dunnell, the big four-engined aircraft was the second of two Lincolns to take part in a fighter affiliation sortie across north-west Europe that day, testing NATO's air defences. The first, flown by Flight Sergeant Denham, had already been subjected to aggressive buzzing by a pair of MiG-15s, even though it was flying within the British zone. The crew returned to Leconfield, shaken though unhurt. However, the situation was about to escalate dramatically.

Two hours after Denham's Lincoln

An Avro Lincoln B1, similar to RF531, peels away from the camera. The Lincoln was developed from the wartime Lancaster and was the last piston-powered bomber to serve with the RAF.

took off from Leconfield, Dunnell's aircraft (RF531), carrying a crew of seven – including Squadron Leader Harold Fitz, the newly appointed commander of 3 Sqn – set out, following the same route.

Whilst flying between Hamburg and West Berlin in Soviet-controlled East Germany, along the designated 20-mile wide air corridor allocated to British aircraft, RF531 apparently veered accidentally out of the air corridor and into East German airspace.

Two MiG-15s soon appeared and fired a warning burst at the aircraft. Realising their mistake, the crew immediately changed course and headed back to the British zone. But one of the Soviet pilots followed up the warning shots by raking the lumbering Lincoln with cannon fire.

Mortally damaged, the burning Lincoln went into a spiral. Of the three crewmen who succeeded in bailing out of the stricken aircraft, the parachute of one failed to deploy while the other two, according to the testimony of several German eyewitnesses on the ground, were shot in a firing pass by one of the MiG pilots whilst drifting helplessly down on their parachutes. The wreckage of the Lincoln was scattered over a wide area, much of it landing just inside the Soviet zone. All seven men aboard the Lincoln perished.

POLITICAL REACTION

The downing of the Lincoln, apparently whilst legitimately flying within West German airspace, sparked a major political storm in Britain. In the House of Commons an incensed Winston Churchill condemned the Soviet action as "a wanton attack" and gave authorisation for British aircraft to open fire if they were again threatened by Soviet aircraft.

A bitter war of words between London and Moscow ensued, the Government immediately firing off a furious note of protest: "[The British Government] protests in the strongest possible terms against this deliberate act of aggression, involving the murder of British airmen." The note went on to call for "those responsible for the outrage [to] be punished."

This was followed by a statement in Parliament by Foreign Secretary Anthony Eden, who said, "Her Majesty's Government takes a grave view of this serious event. Deliberate and unprovoked attacks of this kind by what are supposed to be friendly forces can only be called barbaric."

Moscow responded by insisting that the British aircraft was in Soviet airspace and that their pilots were forced to open fire only after they themselves had been fired on by the Lincoln's gunners.

"The Soviet planes demanded that the trespassing plane should follow them and

The Lincoln entered RAF service in 1945 and the last examples – five operated by 151 Sqn at RAF Watton – were finally retired on March 12, 1963.

The Avro Lincoln operated with a crew of seven consisting of pilot, flight engineer/co-pilot, navigator, wireless operator, front gunner/bomb aimer, dorsal and rear gunners. All seven aboard RF531, including Squadron Leader Harold Fitz, the newly appointed commander of 3 Sqn, perished in the "wanton attack."

A trio of Avro Lincolns captured aloft in a rare colour photograph.

land at the nearest airfield," read the Soviet statement. "The trespassing plane not only failed to submit to this lawful demand but opened fire on the Soviet planes. A Soviet plane was obliged to answer with a warning shot. The trespassing plane, however, continued firing. The Soviet planes were obliged to open fire in return after which the British aircraft began to lose height and fell south-west of Schwerin, on East German territory."

THE TRUTH

But Moscow's version of events was swiftly contradicted by the RAF, who pointed out that the Lincoln's guns were not loaded at the time and refuting Soviet claims that it had been flying in the Soviet zone when the MiGs attacked. Spent ammunition links from the MiG's guns recovered by RAF investigators within the British zone backed up that position.

However, in a statement in the House of Lords on March 17, 1953, Secretary of State for Air William Sidney did concede that the Lincoln had violated Soviet airspace during the course of its flight. "A study of the information now available indicates that the aircraft may, through a navigational error, have accidentally crossed into the Eastern Zone of Germany at some point," he admitted.

"But," he went on, "the evidence of ground observers and the spent cannon shell links from the Russian fighters picked up in our Western Zone prove that the Russians repeatedly fired on the Lincoln and mercilessly destroyed it when it was actually west of, and within, the Allied zonal frontier. The wreck of the aircraft followed in its descent a track which caused it to fall just within the Russian Zone.

Thus it was actually over our zone when first and mortally fired on, and the lives of seven British airmen were callously taken for a navigational mistake in process of correction which could have been dealt with by the usual method of protest and inquiry."

TRAGIC EXERCISE

There have long been rumours that the Lincoln – a type often used at the time by the RAF on ELINT flights – was possibly on an intelligence gathering mission, perhaps testing Soviet air defences, when it was intercepted and shot down. But according to Intelligence historian Richard Aldrich this was probably not the case. "…The RAF Lincoln lost on March 12, 1953 was not directly involved in radio warfare or special duties," he stated. "It was merely on exercise, and wandered out of one of the defined twenty-mile air corridors over the Soviet Zone between West Germany and Berlin."

He adds, however, that "while the Lincoln had not been on an intelligence flight, its progress was being carefully tracked by a British SIGINT unit on the ground at RAF Scharfoldendorf in the British zone of Germany."

While refusing to accept full responsibility, Moscow did issue an 'expression of regret' upon returning the bodies of the crew to RAF Celle. Six of the crew – Squadron Leader Fitz, Flight Lieutenant Stephen Wyles and Sergeants Ronald Stevens, George Long, William Mason and Kenneth Jones – were repatriated to the UK and buried with full military honours on March 19, 1953 in St Catherine's Churchyard, close to their base in Leconfield. The pilot, Peter Dunnell, was buried in Colton Churchyard, Norfolk.

But other RAF aircraft certainly were engaged in intelligence gathering flights around – and indeed over – the Iron Curtain at the time. Just five months after the Lincoln shoot-down a Canberra of 540 Sqn was reportedly intercepted and slightly damaged by MiG fighters while apparently on a photo-reconnaissance mission over the Soviet Union.

Thankfully, however, never again would the RAF lose an aircraft to Soviet fighters over the Iron Curtain. ❖

SUBSCRIBE
TO YOUR FAVOURITE MAGAZINE
AND SAVE

Officially The World's Number One Military Aviation Magazine...
Published monthly, AirForces Monthly is devoted entirely to modern military aircraft and their air arms. It has built up a formidable reputation worldwide by reporting from places not generally covered by other military magazines. Its world news is the best around, covering all aspects of military aviation, region by region; offering features on the strengths of the world's air forces, their conflicts, weaponry and exercises.

key.aero/airforces-monthly

GREAT SUBSCRIPTION OFFERS FROM

For the Best in Modern Military and Commercial Aviation...
Over the years, AIR International has established an unrivalled reputation for authoritative reporting across the full spectrum of aviation subjects. With more pages than ever, all still dedicated to commercial and military aviation, we have correspondents and top aviation writers from around the world, offering exciting news, detailed and informative features and stunning photography in each monthly issue.

key.aero/air-international

America's Best-Selling Military Aviation Magazine...
With in-depth editorial coverage alongside the finest imagery from the world's foremost aviation photographers, Combat Aircraft is the world's favourite military aviation magazine. With thought-provoking opinion pieces, detailed information and rare archive imagery, Combat Aircraft is your one-stop-source of military aviation news and features from across the globe.

key.aero/combataircraft

VISIT KEY.AERO
your online home for historic aviation

 Order direct or subscribe at:
shop.keypublishing.com

 Or call UK **01780 480404**
Overseas **+44 1780 480404**
Lines open 9.00-5.30, Monday-Friday

MiG-31 *Foxhound*
– Russia's Game Changer

MiG-31 '903' at low-level over the Russian countryside in the late 1990s.

Dr Dave Sloggett explores the transformative effect the MiG-31 had on the Russian Air Force when the supersonic interceptor was introduced into service

The MiG-31 aircraft (NATO reporting name *Foxhound*) is a thoroughbred of the air-to-air interceptor world. As a supersonic interceptor it is one of the fastest combat jets in the world. It is an aircraft that puts the design teams in the modern day Mikoyan Design Bureau at the forefront of many technologies that are the envy of the West.

When it first appeared in the inventory of the Russian Air Force it added several new dimensions to the air defence of the then Soviet Union. It can be said to have been a transformational weapon system – one that introduced entirely new paradigms in the way the Soviet Union and subsequently Russia managed its air space. Today 252 remain on strength from the original 519 built, although only around 130 are operated at any one time by the Russian Air Force. Russian Naval Aviation is thought to have a further 32 on strength, as does the Kazakhstan Air Force.

PERFORMANCE PARAMETERS

While not strictly regarded as a traditional dog-fighter, the MiG-31's combination of speed and range enabled it to operate over much wider areas than its predecessor, the MiG-25 *Foxbat*. The *Foxhound* is an interceptor that is a platform for long-range missiles, not for close-in engagements.

High fidelity simulations of the aerodynamics of the MiG-31 suggest, for example, that it would perform badly in a dog-fight against an F-15. It can only pull 5G when flown at supersonic speeds. However, that was not what it was designed for as an airframe.

The interceptor was intended to scramble quickly, close with an enemy far away from Russian territory at speed, detect them over over the radar horizon and destroy it before disengaging – a capability that has become increasingly important as the range of cruise missiles has grown.

The ability for an aircraft platform, like the B-1B or the venerable B-52, to stand off and deliver weapons requires that it remains unseen while it penetrates Russian airspace to launch cruise missiles in a conflict situation. The MiG-31 is tasked to engage and prevent that occurring. In a world where he who fires first is thought to succeed, the issue for the Russia Air Defence system is how to defeat the stealth technologies favoured by the US so that incoming threats can be detected and handed off to the MiG-31 to engage.

The MiG-31's other performance parameters are very impressive. Using the afterburning thrust of its two 34,172lb/thrust Soloviev D-30F6 turbofans the MiG-31 requires 1,189m (3,900ft) of runway to get airborne and can land in 793m (2,600ft). Climbing out on full reheat it can reach 34,000ft (1,036m) in eight minutes. A minute later it is able to reach 65,000ft (1,981m). Its combat ceiling is 67,600ft (20,604m), similar to that of its predecessor. It can achieve airspeeds of Mach 2.83 and operate over a range of 1,864 miles (3,000km). Drop-tanks extend this range to 3,355 miles (5,400km).

The addition of in-flight refuelling adds other dimensions, allowing Russia to also operate Combat Air Patrols (CAP) – something that has traditionally eluded the Soviet Air Force.

For the defence of Russia, a country with various climatic regions and a shared-border that extends to 12,577 miles (20,241km) – only China has a longer border – and covers 16 sovereign countries, the long-range MiG-31 was an ideal solution.

HIGH ARCTIC OPERATIONS

Its operations in the Arctic region, with its ability to be refuelled in-flight, have seen packages of *Foxhounds* extend their operations to the North Pole. On July 30, 1987, a MiG-31 having refuelled twice reached the top of the world in what was a 6.5-hour flight. For the USSR this was a first and in 1989 production of 101 air-refuelling capable MiG-31DZ variants began.

Today, as Russia extends its influence over the High Arctic opening bases across the Tundra and islands that litter the edges of the Arctic Ocean, the MiG-31 provides the ability to escort long-range bombers – such as the Tupolev Tu-95 and the Tu-160 – across large-swathes of the Arctic Ocean, dominating an area vital to the future Russian economy. This increased flexibility has seen the return of scouting missions towards the UK resume, with MiG-31 interceptors accompanying Russian bombers now carrying even longer-range stand-off missiles capable of attacking RAF bases. In the past it

In July 2015 RAF Typhoons were scrambled from Estonia as part of their Baltic Air Policing mission intercept MiG-31 *Foxhounds*. The alert was the single largest intercept British aircrew performed in the region and as well as the MiGs the Russian formation included four Sukhoi Su-34 fighters and two Antonov An-26 transport aircraft. The aircraft were closely followed by the Typhoons as they flew from Russia towards the enclave of Kaliningrad. Days earlier Norwegian F-16 fighters stationed in Lithuania were scrambled to intercept a large formation of Russian aircraft that included four MiG-31s, four Sukhoi Su-24 fighters, two Antonov An-26 and one Ilyushin Il-76 transport aircraft. The aircraft appeared to be flying as part of a training mission but had turned off their transponders. *Ministry of Defence*

◀ The prototype MiG-31 – seen here – first flew on September 16, 1975. The type entered serial production in 1979 and entered service on May 6, 1981. During testing a re-engined version of the *Foxhound* set a number of new world records. In 1977, in the hands of famous MiG test pilot Alexander Fedotov it reached an absolute maximum altitude of 123,510ft and set a time-to-height record to 115,000ft in 4 minutes and 11.78 seconds. His deputy, Pyotr Ostapenko, set a time-to-height record to 98,000ft in 3 minutes and 9.8 seconds. *All MiGAvia/Russian Aircraft Corporation unless stated*

was the bombers the RAF had to worry about. Today it is sophisticated packages comprising the Tu-160, Tu-95 and Tu-22 bombers escorted by MiG-31 and other Russian aircraft that comprise an evolving threat.

DEVELOPMENTS AND UPGRADES

Given the impact the *Foxhound* has had on the operation of the Russian Air Force, it is not difficult to see why current planning assumptions are based on the MiG-31 remaining in service at least until the middle of the 2030s and possibly beyond. For an aircraft that first flew in 1975 and went out of production in 1994, that is an impressive service life – albeit one punctuated by many upgrades and the introduction of new powerplants and electronics into the airframe.

To address the intercept of low-flying cruise missiles, an Infra-Red Search and Track (IRST) sensor system with a reported range of 25 miles (40km) was added to the electronics systems on the MiG-31's platform.

Other new electronic developments provided a higher degree of autonomy of operations by reducing reliance on ground-based controllers and radars with detection limits imposed by the radar horizon.

The introduction of the MiG-31 with its Phazotron Zaslon (which in Russian means 'barrier') S-800 passively-steered electronic array radar system, which was originally unveiled at the 1991 Paris Air Salon alongside the MiG-31, provided an ability to break free of the constraints of ground-based radar systems and mirrored emerging Western doctrines in

> **" Today it is sophisticated packages comprising the Tu-160, Tu-95 and Tu-22 bombers escorted by MiG-31 and other Russian aircraft that comprise an evolving threat "**

the air defence arena. It was the first time a phased array radar system had been installed in a jet fighter (and would not be repeated until 2000 when Mitsubishi introduced its J/APG-1 radar into service on the F-2 fighter).

Russian offers to fly the MiG-31 against an F-117 Nighthawk stealth fighter also at the Paris Air Salon were dismissed by the Americans as a publicity stunt but to remove any doubt about the MiG's capabilities, the Russians somewhat uncharacteristically removed the radome to allow the unique construction of the radar to be seen.

The Zaslon radar is an all-weather, pulse-doppler, multimode airborne radar system known in NATO circles by its codename *Flash Dance*. The radar is built from two separate electronically-scanned arrays: the X-band primary detection radar which is made from 17,00 emitters operates alongside an L-Band transponder array made up of 64 emitters. The original 1.1m diameter antenna was held in position with a scanning sector of +/-70 degrees in azimuth and elevation. Using the phased array elements, the beam can be constructed and moved in 1.2m/s.

The original S-800 (Zaslon-A) was stated to have a target detection range of 124 miles (200km) against a target with a

▲ The MiG-31 was one of the highlights of the 1991 Paris Air Salon. Russian offers to fly the MiG-31 against an F-117 Nighthawk stealth fighter were dismissed by the Americans as a publicity stunt but to remove any doubt about the MiG's capabilities, the Russians somewhat uncharacteristically removed the radome to allow the unique construction of the radar to be seen. *KEY- Duncan Cubitt*

▶ The *Foxhound* is a big aeroplane that weighs in at 101,900lbs at maximum take-off weight.

The Russian Air Force is reported to have over 250 Foxhounds and the Russian Defence Ministry expects the type to remain in service until the 2030s.

radar cross section of 19m² (such as an AWACS). It also featured a look-down, shoot-down capability to engage cruise missiles in flight.

The radar is reported to be capable of tracking ten targets in parallel whilst engaging four. A variant of the radar, the Zaslon-M, is reported to have 50% to 100% improved performance over earlier variants and can track 24 targets at the

> " Current planning assumptions are based on the MiG-31 remaining in service at least until the middle of the 2030s "

same time and engage six simultaneously. In a demonstration firing in April 1994, an R-37 missile fired from a MiG-31 was able to engage and destroy a target at a range of 186 miles (300km).

THE 'WOLFPACK'
The deployment of the radar system on the MiG-31 also introduced the idea that the responsibility for managing engagements could be transferred to the Weapon Systems Operator (WSO) in the back seat. This gave the MiG-31 greater autonomy and an ability to cooperate with other aircraft more swiftly in engaging high-speed incoming targets. For what was often seen to be an antiquated Russian Air Defence system that was hugely centralised, this was transformational. Four MiG-31s operating as a 'wolfpack' could cover a frontal area of 560 mile (900km), sharing their radar pictures with each other and a commander flying as one of the WSOs could allocate inbound targets to specific aircraft. The simple-to-operate radar system made life very easy for the WSO and accounts of how it was able to autonomously plan and execute parallel engagements with minimal involvement appear in many transcripts documenting the history of the MiG-31.

Naturally such a step-change in the Russian air defence capability drew a great deal of interest from Western intelligence agencies. When evidence emerged that the capabilities of the Russian electronics packages on the MiG-31 had been compromised by a spy working deep inside the Russian Ministry of Defence, improvements and upgrades to maintain the effectiveness of the MiG-31 where quickly forthcoming.

In addition to updates of the electronics packages on the MiG-31, the Russians also introduced a glass cockpit. Today the Zaslon radar system is believed to be capable of acquiring and tracking targets over a range of up to 160 miles (257km), although its effectiveness against the stealthy ultra-low radar cross sections of the F-22, F-35 and B-2 aircraft remains unclear. That challenge will only increase as the Americans develop and roll out the new B-21 bomber to replace the B-2 Spirit in the mid-2020s. This explains, in part, why Russia is working so hard to develop the next generation of its Airborne Early Warning (AEW) aircraft, which will work alongside the MiG-31.

NEW WEAPON SYSTEMS
Any air defence analyst will say that there is little point in being able to detect an enemy far away if you cannot engage it quickly. Over the horizon engagements are now de-rigour in the air defence world and to achieve that the MiG-31 armaments have been upgraded. Coming from a long series of missiles whose development started in the late 1960s, the R-33S (NATO Codename AA-9 *Amos*) is reported to be as capable as the AIM-54 Phoenix missile system that was operated by the US Navy on the F-14 Tomcat aircraft. The range of the missile has steadily increased in service: originally 75 miles (120km), today it is reported to exceed 186 miles (300km). It flies at speeds between Mach 4.5 and Mach 6, and uses a combination

The MiG-31 is powered by a pair of Soloviev D-30F6 afterburning turbofans that produce 20,900lb/thrust each in dry power and 34,172lb/thrust in reheat. *Russian Air Force*

of semi-active radar homing for initial target acquisition and mid-course updates with inertial navigation to home onto the target at extreme range. It main prey are American bombers, such as the B-1B and the B-52.

The R-33 is part of a mixed package of missiles carried by the MiG-31. These include the shorter-range R-60 infra-red homing missile which is proximity fused (NATO codename AA-8 *Aphid*). This has a reported operational range of 5 miles (8km). Two Bisnovat R-40TD1 Medium-range missiles can also be carried to provide a suite of options to the WSO. The MiG-31 also has a six-barrel 30mm internal canon capability with 800 rounds of ammunition. It can fire this at 10,000 rounds per minute and can therefore engage targets for just under five seconds. To perform anti-satellite duties two aircraft were adapted to the MiG-31D variant. These aircraft had ballast in the nose instead of radars, a flat fuselage under-surface (i.e. no recessed weapon system bays) and large winglets above and below the wing-tips. They were equipped with Vympel ASAT missiles but the project never got beyond the prototype stage.

" Russian offers to fly the MiG-31 against an F-117 Nighthawk stealth fighter also at the Paris air show were dismissed by the Americans as a publicity stunt "

NEW PARADIGMS
The autonomy introduced by the capabilities of the *Foxhound* provided an opportunity to fundamentally re-think the operation of the Soviet air defence system – a new paradigm for the Soviet and subsequently Russian air defence systems. The combination of these two developments allowed the MiG-31 to track and engage four targets simultaneously.

This was a significant step from the single target tracking and engagement facility available to the MiG-25. Recent developments have also seen the MiG-31 inter-operate with the Sukhoi Su-27 *Flanker*. As the new Russian Beriev AEW-100, which is based on the Ilyushin Il-76MD-90A and flew in November 2017, enters service and replaces the Beriev A-50 *Mainstay* as Russia's primary AWACS aircraft, the ways of operating the MiG-31 will no doubt evolve again.

▼ To perform anti-satellite duties two aircraft were adapted to the MiG-31D variant. These aircraft had ballast in the nose instead of radars, flat fuselage under-surface (i.e. no recessed weapon system bays) and large winglets above and below the wing-tips. They were equipped with Vympel ASAT missiles but the project never got beyond the prototype stage. *KEY Collection*

◄ A pair of MiG-31s formate at altitude. The type was not used during Russia's recent involvement in the war in Syria and although the Syrian Air Force ordered eight MiG-31E aircraft in 2007 the order was suspended in 2009. In 2015, the media reported that six MiG-31s had been delivered to Syria but Russia has denied making the deliveries. *Russian Air Force*

The MiG-31 has been in service since 1981 but there seems to be no sign of the sun setting on the career of the mighty *Foxhound*.
Dmitry Pichugin via COAP Media

The front and rear cockpits of a Russian Air Force MiG-31 *Foxhound*.

ENGAGING BLACKBIRD

The various developments employed by the MiG-31 in the 1980s enabled Soviet air defence systems to take another leap in capabilities similar to that enjoyed in the early 1960s when the Gary Powers incident saw a Russian interceptor shoot-down a U-2 spyplane. In the wake of the first Russian satellite launch and the first cosmonaut, American spy agencies worried that the US was lagging Soviet defence developments. The U-2 compounded that problem and for the United States Air Force (USAF) the subsequent trial and revelations of connections between the aircraft and the Central Intelligence Agency (CIA) was a huge embarrassment and the political fallout was significant.

The USAF enjoyed a period of relative immunity from the Soviet and then Russian Air Force interceptor capabilities when the U-2s were replaced by the Lockheed SR-71 Blackbird aircraft. The Blackbird's ability to fly at more than three and a half times the speed of sound at 88,000ft (26,822m) combined with its small radar cross section and electronic countermeasures equipment gave it a sense of invincibility.

However, the aura surrounding the SR-71 was shattered on January 31, 1986 when MiG-31 Captain Mikhail Myagkiy and his WSO were able to lock onto a SR-71 when flying 75 miles (120km) away at 52,000ft (15,850m). After climbing to 65,676ft (20,018m) the aircrew were able to visually identify the SR-71. Speaking after the event Captain Myagkiy noted that "had the SR-71 violated Soviet airspace, a live missile launch would have been carried out. There was practically no chance the aircraft could have avoided an R-33 missile".

This was not the only time such an intercept occurred. Six months later over the Barents Sea a single SR-71 was intercepted by six MiG-31 aircraft that performed a co-ordinated intercept on the target covering six separate angles of attack, any one of which would have resulted in the SR-71 being shot down. This specific event showed the power of the 'wolfpack' in action.

Chastened by this event the USAF did not conduct any further overflights of Soviet or subsequently Russian airspace. Indeed, these two events have been used by some commentators to suggest that they were the catalyst that saw the swift retirement from service of the SR-71 and the continued development of the Mach 6-capable SR-72. This latest development in American Intelligence, Surveillance, Target Acquisition and Reconnaissance (ISTAR) platform is likely to remain safe for some time until hypersonic missiles are added into the inventory of the MiG-31 armaments.

STILL A PLAYER

While plans for the replacement of the MiG-31 were announced in 2015, the new airframe is unlikely to enter service until the middle of the 2030s. Until such time as that happens, the MiG-31 will continue to be

A Russian Air Force MiG-31 is prepared for flight.

Left: Climbing out on full reheat the MiG-31 can reach 34,000ft in eight minutes. A minute later it is able to reach 65,000ft. Its combat ceiling is 67,600ft. *Dmitry Pichugin via COAP Media* **Right:** With the brake 'chute streaming in the breeze a MiG-31 returns from a training sortie. *Dmitry Pichugin via COAP Media*

the backbone of the Russian Air Defence system.

Recent deployments into northern Russia to enable the MiG-31 to reinforce Russia's expansive claims to the High Arctic show that the aircraft remains a significant player in Russian air defence thinking. Developments around the Anti-Access Area Denial (A2AD) technologies epitomised by the introduction of the S-400 missile system and its replacement the S-500 show that the day of the interceptor has not passed.

Operationally, the MiG-31 has not been used in Syria by the Russians. Syrian Air Force MiG-25s have struggled to make an impact in the conflict and the Russians also had to consider how operating the MiG-31 in the full face of the Israeli intelligence collection capabilities might see important operating parameters compromised.

That the MiG-31 has not been offered on the export market, unlike its predecessor, is also perhaps surprising but in this way it maintains its mystique.

If there is a blemish on the *Foxhound's* career it is that it has never been used in anger. How it would perform in war against a peer enemy like the USA or China remains open to doubt.

While claims emerging from former MiG-31 pilots suggesting that it would be a match for the F-22s in the American inventory may be subject to some hyperbole, there is little to doubt that the MiG-31 still has a lot to give. Like any thoroughbred it will have had its day at some point in the future. That, however, appears to be many years away. ❖

Left: Today it is sophisticated packages comprising the Tu-160, Tu-95 and Tu-22 bombers escorted by MiG-31 and other Russian aircraft that comprise an evolving threat. *Russian Air Force* **Right:** A Russian Navy MiG-31 operates from Kamchatka in December 2016. *Russian Air Force*

The MiG-AT promised much and had great export potential but lost out to the Yak-130.

21ˢᵀ Century MiG

Despite its prominence in the 1970s and 80s the MiG Design Bureau has failed to win any major aircraft tenders in the post-Soviet era, but this is not for the want of creating some truly memorable and promising designs, as Steve Bridgewater reveals.

The MiG 1.44 on static display at the MAKS Airshow in Moscow. The aircraft is thought to have only flown twice.

Despite tens of thousands of aircraft rolling off the Mikoyan-Gurevich production line since the 1940s the talented design bureau has failed to deliver in recent years.

In 1964 Mikhail Gurevich retired and Artem Mikoyan died six years later in 1970. He was succeeded as chief designer by Rostislav A Belyakov and in 1978 the company was renamed simply as the Mikoyan OKB.

In 1995 the Mikoyan OKB was merged with two production facilities to form the Moscow Aviation Production Association MiG – becoming the Russian Aircraft Corporation MiG (RAC MiG) in 2006 when the Russian government merged Mikoyan's shares with Ilyushin, Irkut, Sukhoi, Tupolev, and Yakovlev. RAC MiG is part of the United Aircraft Corporation and Mikoyan and Sukhoi were placed within the same UAC operating unit.

In recent years RAC MiG has produced little in the way of completely new designs and in 1999 Nikolai Nikitin was appointed the corporation's General Director and General Designer. Sources suggest Nikitin focused most of the company's resources on the development of the passenger aircraft at the expense of military development, a move that allegedly prompted the resignation in December 1999 of many of its leading military aircraft designers, including the chief designers and their deputies for the MiG-29 and MiG-31 programmes.

Nikitin was replaced by Valery Toryanin in November 2003, who was in turn replaced by Alexey Fedorov in September 2004. The following year, under Federov's

> "RAC MiG began production of new 'Generation 4++' aircraft"

guidance, RAC MiG began production of a new unified family of multi-role fighters based on the basic MiG-29 and MiG-31 airframes. Described as 'Generation 4++' aircraft the new fighters will form the basis of RAC MiG's product line for the foreseeable future.

FIFTH GENERATION JET

MiG's last attempt to create an entirely new fighter began in the 1980s and was intended as the company's first Fifth Generation fighter.

Codenamed Project 1.44/1.42 the aircraft was envisaged as the USSR's answer to the US Advanced Tactical Fighter (ATF) programme – which led to the F-22 Raptor.

The definition of a Fifth Generation fighter is vague but they are generally considered to require some aspect of stealth technology as well as high-performance airframes, advanced avionics and highly integrated computer systems capable of networking with other elements within the battlespace for situation awareness.

Faced with the prospect of the USAF having access to squadrons of super-manoeuvrable and stealthy F-22s, the Soviet government tasked its fighter design bureaus with developing a replacement for its MiG-29 *Fulcrum* and Sukhoi Su-27 *Flanker* aircraft.

While Sukhoi concentrated on the S-37 programme, later designated Su-47, MiG occupied itself with two projects: one focused on a heavy multi-role design designated MFI (Mnogofunksionalni Frontovoy Istrebitel or 'Multifunctional Frontline Fighter'), and another aiming to produce a light tactical fighter named LFI (Lyogkiy Frontovoy Istrebitel or 'Light Frontline Fighter'). Other LFI entries included the Yakovlev Yak-43 (an upgraded and more-stealthy version of the VTOL Yak-41 *Freestyle*) and the Sukhoi S-37.

The MiG 1.44 *Flatpack* was Mikoyan's attempt to create a Fifth Generation fighter for the Russian Air Force.

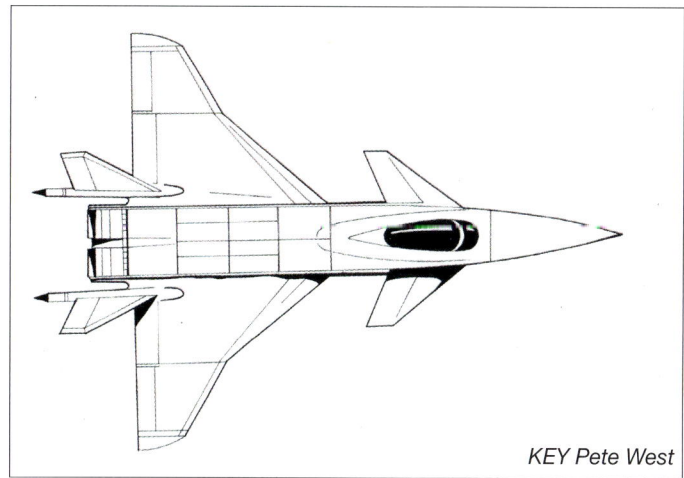

KEY Pete West

The unusual planform of the MiG 1.44 bears some resemblance to the Typhoon and Rafale, albeit with a much smaller wing.

The second MiG-AT demonstrator flew in camouflage to emphasise the type's planned combat role.

In order to minimise costs Mikoyan's MFI and LFI entries were to share as many components as possible, but as the development progressed it soon became obvious that working on two complex projects was proving costly.

CANARDS

Nonetheless, Mikoyan proceeded with the preliminary design phase of both the MFI and LFI with assistance from the TsAGI (Tsentralniy Aerogidrodinamicheskiy Institut or 'Central Aero- and Hydrodynamic Institute') – the latter responsible for wind tunnel testing and aerodynamic studies.

The TsAGI recommended Mikoyan proceed with an aircraft that included a delta wing and canard fore-planes, as these were felt to improve both lift and agility, especially in a fly-by-wire aircraft that was naturally unstable and kept 'in trim' by complex computers. Subsequent testing by TsAGI with radio controlled models revealed that the design would still be controllable at high angles of attack up to 60 degrees.

The MFI variant evolved into a design not too dissimilar to the Eurofighter Typhoon and Dassault Rafale but it was also expected to incorporate vectored thrust technologies similar to the F-22 Raptor.

In 1987, Mikoyan and the associated institutions submitted the MFI and LFI proposals for review. Both aircraft passed the review process but for budgetary reasons Mikoyan shelved the lightweight fighter in order to free up resources for the MFI.

For the next few years the aircraft – now dubbed Project 1.42 – progressed under the leadership of Chief Project Engineer Gheogiy A Sedov. The aircraft would now need to be a multi-role fighter – fulfilling both air-to-air missions planned for the LFI and the original MFI air-to-ground missions.

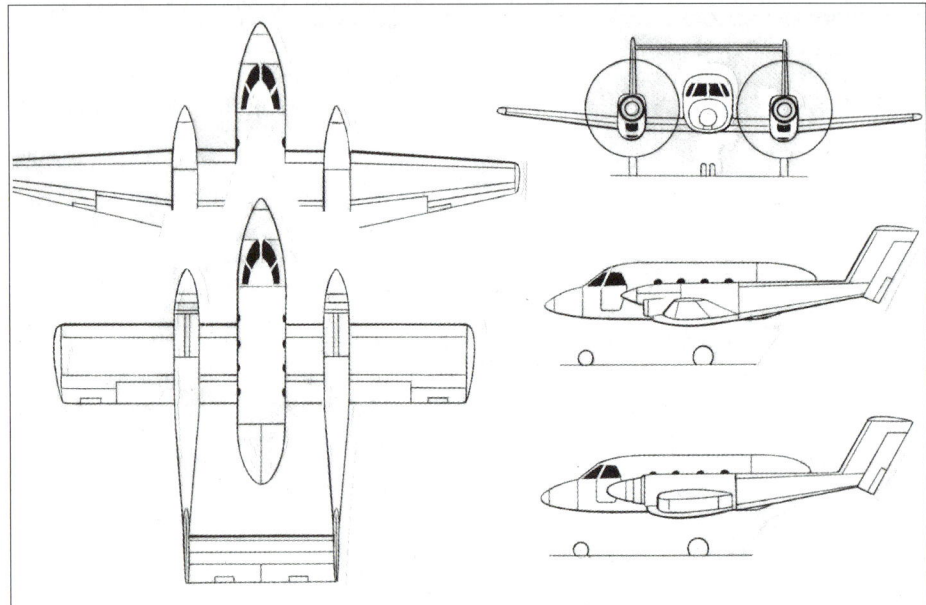

The MiG-110 was a stillborn attempt at creating a multi-purpose cargo and passenger aircraft. *KEY Pete West*

The design the team settled upon was a delta-winged aircraft with twin fins and a close-coupled canard layout which, when working with the vectored thrust and fly-by-wire controls, promised to give the fighter excellent manoeuvrability. Mikoyan made use of weight-saving materials in the construction of the aircraft with aluminium-lithium alloys making up 35% of the empty weight and composites contributing another 30%

In order to make the jet 'stealthy' Mikoyan's designers minimised surface-area and used radar-absorbent materials. The weapons would also be carried internally to reduce the radar cross section.

Power would come from a pair of 39,020lb/thrust afterburning Lyulka Saturn AL-41F turbofans, giving the fighter a projected top speed of Mach 2.35 and the ability to supercruise (fly supersonically without the need for afterburner). The thrust could also be vectored in both pitch and yaw planes.

The aircraft was fitted with a fully glass cockpit and a Pulse-Doppler N014 radar that had a range of 260 miles (420km) and could track 40 targets simultaneously and engage 20 of them.

FINDING FUNDING

In 1988 Mikoyan was issued with a specific operational requirement for the 1.42 and in 1991 the proposed design passed the Soviet Air Force's critical review, paving the way for the construction of a flyable technology demonstrator, referred to as the Type 1.44.

The aircraft would be used to verify the aerodynamic layout and flight control system of the design and construction was about half complete when the collapse of the Soviet Union brought a halt to funding.

In an attempt to attract financial backing, Mikoyan lobbied the government to declassify the aircraft, which would enable it to be promoted at airshows. However, the new Russian government refused.

Development continued at a snail's pace on the rare occasions that funding could be sourced and in 1994 the incomplete aircraft was transported to Zhukovsky airfield near Moscow for ground tests. The year ended with Mikoyan's Chief Test Pilot Roman Taskaev carrying out Project 1.44's first high-speed runs but just as the tempo of testing increased, the programme was postponed again as Mikoyan did not have sufficient funds to purchase the components needed to make the demonstrator flyable.

The entire project was therefore postponed indefinitely and in 1997 the Russian government cancelled production of the design due to its unacceptably high unit cost.

The next few years were difficult for the Mikoyan Design Bureau but eventual changes in management opened up other sources of funding. The change in management structure also resulted in the Russian government's decision to eventually reveal the existence of the project in December 1998.

The following year the Type 1.44 – by now given the NATO reporting name *Flatpack* – returned to testing following an official roll-out ceremony at Zhukovsky on January 12, 1999. Ground and taxi testing went well and on February 29, 2000 the new fighter finally performed its maiden flight. Vladimir Gorboonov was at the helm for the 18-minute flight during which the 1.44 reached 3,300ft and a speed of 320kts (370mph).

CANCELLED

Gorboonov later described the aircraft as "docile" but it did not fly again until April 27 and that 22-minute flight appears to have been its final sortie. The programme has since been cancelled, with the sole prototype now residing at Gromov Flight Research Institute.

In 2015 the aircraft was refurbished and exhibited statically at the MAKS airshow in Zhukovsky, leading some to question if the airframe is to play a part in Mikoyan's entry into the Russian LMFS contest. The Liogkiy Mnogofunktsionalniy Frontovoi Samolyet (Light Multi-Function Frontal Aircraft) programme calls for a stealthy, single-engined multirole combat aircraft to replace the MiG-29.

Though not a participant in the original MFI programme, Sukhoi started its own programme to develop technologies for a Fifth Generation fighter aircraft in the early 1990s. The result was the S-37 (later referred to as the Su-47 and now the Su-57).

Following the cancellation of the MiG 1.44 Russia began a new search for a next-generation fighter. The winner of the PAK-FA (Perspektivny Aviatsionny Kompleks Frontovoy Aviatsii or 'Prospective Aviation Complex of Frontline Aviation') contract was judged to be the Sukhoi Su-57 and the type is expected to enter service in 2018.

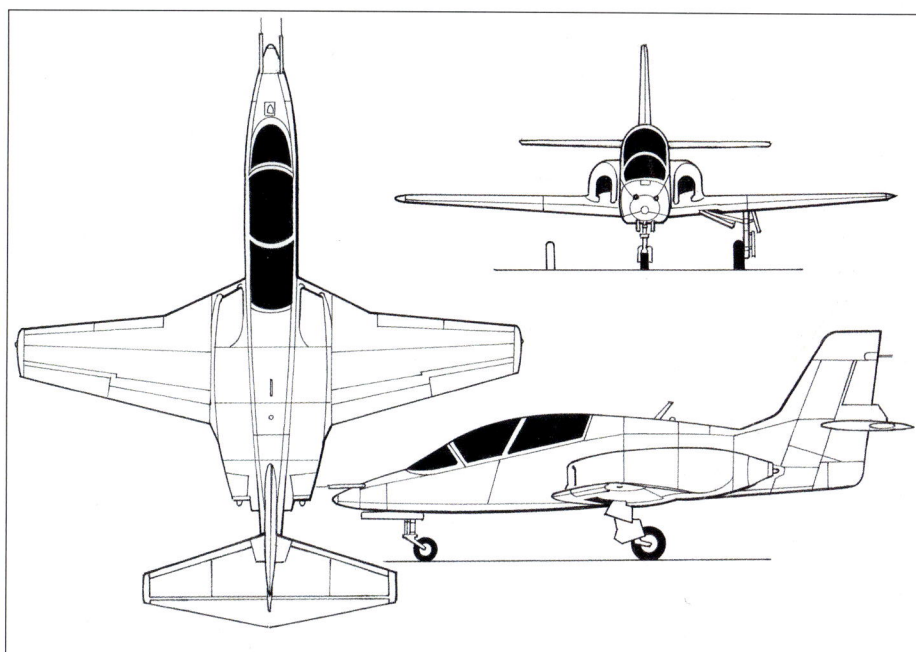

The MiG-AT was a conventional-looking armed trainer. Power came from Western engines and the project was the first Russian/Western collaboration to reach a maiden flight. *KEY Pete West*

CARGO AIRCRAFT

Another stillborn project was the MiG-110, which entered development in 1995 as a proposed passenger/cargo aircraft. It would have been a high-mounted cantilever monoplane with a pod-and-boom configuration with a clamshell rear fuselage. Power was to come from two Klimov TV7-117 turboprop engines and the aircraft was to be manufactured in four variants – the MiG-110N dedicated passenger version, a MiG-110NP paramilitary version, a MiG-110M combination passenger/freight version and a MiG-110A variant to be produced under licence in Austria. Sadly the aircraft never got beyond the drawing board.

MiG-AT

Mikoyan's other major project of the 1990s and 2000s was the MiG-AT advanced trainer and light attack aircraft. It was designed as a replacement for the ubiquitous Aero L-29 and L-39 trainers in service with the Russian Air Force and air arms of countless former Soviet Bloc nations.

The MiG-AT was the first joint aircraft development programme between Russia and the West (France in particular) to reach first flight.

The aircraft was competing for business with the Yakovlev Yak-130 and, besides the Russian Air Force and Air Defence Forces, Mikoyan sought to export the armed trainer to India, South Africa, Greece, France and former Soviet states such as Kazakhstan and Uzbekistan.

Compared to the Yak-130 the MiG-AT was a much more conventional airframe. It had a low-set straight wing, a mid-mounted tail and a pair of French-built 3,237lb/thrust SNECMA Turbomeca Larzac engines mounted on either side of the fuselage.

The aircraft first flew in March 1996, the seven-minute test sortie taking place at Zhukovsky.

The MiG-AT had a digital three-channel quadruple redundant Avionika KSU-821 fly-by-wire system which allowed its characteristics to be modified in order to simulate the flight behaviour of different classes of aircraft (from agile fighter to heavy ground attack machines).

Training manoeuvres included sustained turns to a limit of +8G and pilots could be schooled in interception and combat manoeuvring including directed interceptions, close combat and long-range attack manoeuvres.

The combat trainer version of the aircraft, the MiG-ATC, could also be equipped with a multimode radar and systems suite for launching guided and unguided weapons for combat training against air, ground and sea targets. The jet had nine hardpoints for carrying up to 4,410lbs (2,000kg) of external stores including gun packs, bombs, rockets and guided and unguided missiles including the R-73E, R-77 or AIM-9L Sidewinder.

However, in April 2002, Commander-in-Chief Vladimir Mikhailov stated that the Yak-130 had been chosen as the Russian Air Force's new trainer. It was felt to be superior to the MiG-AT, which was subsequently cancelled after just two prototypes had been produced.

Today the Mikoyan company concentrates on refurbishing existing MiG fighters for current operators and refining versions of the MiG-29 and MiG-31 for prospective purchasers. However, with such a history in producing war winning aircraft one can only hope that the manufacturer returns to prominence in due course. ❖

MUSEUM MiGs

Of the thousands built, large numbers of MiGs have been preserved over the past decades - although the jets remain a rarity in UK museums. Jamie Ewan presents a roundup of those on display in Britain.

TYPE	SERIAL	LOCATION
Mikoyan-Gurevich MiG-15UTI *Fagot**	'309'	Museum of Flight, East Fortune
Mikoyan-Gurevich MiG-15 *Fagot* (PZL Mielec Lim-2)	1120	RAF Museum Cosford, Shrops
Mikoyan-Gurevich MiG-15 *Fagot* (PZL Mielec Lim-2)	'1420' (G-BMZF)	Fleet Air Arm Museum, Yeovilton, Somerset
Mikoyan-Gurevich MiG-15 *Fagot* (Aero Vodochody Aero S-103)	3677	Museum of Flight, East Fortune, Scotland
Mikoyan-Gurevich MiG-15 *Fagot* (Aero Vodochody Aero S-103)	'1972'	Norfolk & Suffolk Aviation Museum, Suffolk
Mikoyan-Gurevich MiG-17 *Fresco* (PZL Mielec Lim-5)	'1211' (G-MIGG)	North Weald, Essex
Mikoyan-Gurevich MiG-21PF *Fishbed-D*	501	IWM Duxford, Cambs
Mikoyan-Gurevich MiG-21SPS *Fishbed-D*	959	Midland Air Musuem, Coventry
Mikoyan-Gurevich MiG-21PF *Fishbed-D*	503 (G-BRAM)	RAF Museum Cosford, Shrops
Mikoyan-Gurevich MiG-21UM *Mongol**	'0446'	Thameside Aviation Museum, Essex
Mikoyan-Gurevich MiG-23ML *Flogger*	'458'	Newark Air Museum, Notts
Mikoyan-Gurevich MiG-27K *Flogger-J*	'71'	Newark Air Museum, Notts
Mikoyan-Gurevich MiG-27K *Flogger-J*	'23'	Hawarden Air Services, Hawarden, Chester
Mikoyan-Gurevich MiG-29 *Fulcrum**	526	Fenland Aviation Museum, Cambs

*Front fuselage

Hawarden Air Services has two MiG-27s in the UK, including MiG-27K *Flogger-J* 'Red 71' which is on loan to Newark Air Museum and displayed at its Nottinghamshire site.

The RAF Museum's MiG-21PF was built for the Hungarian Air Force but acquired by Aces High Ltd in 1989 and brought to the UK as a film prop. It was registered G-BRAM and ground run at North Weald, Essex but never flown. It later passed through the Bournemouth Aviation Museum and Farnborough Air Sciences Trust before being acquired by the RAFM in 2006 and going on display in the National Cold War Exhibition building following repainting in its original markings.

Cold War Foes. Former Hungarian Air Force MiG-21PF *Fishbed-D* '501' is on display at the Imperial War Museum, Duxford alongside a former RAF McDonnell Douglas F-4 Phantom II. *All Steve Bridgewater unless stated*

Left: Now on display at the Midland Air Museum at Coventry Airport this former East German Air Force MiG-21SPS was imported into the UK in the 1990s by the Duxford-based Old Flying Machine Company. It is seen here being repainted into its original markings during an overhaul. **Middle:** MiG-23-ML *Flogger* 'Red 458' belongs to Hawarden Air Services but is on loan to and on display at the Newark Air Museum. It is the only example of its type in the UK.
Right: The Museum of Flight at East Fortune, Scotland features an example of the Aero S-103/MiG-15 that was flown by the Czechoslovakian 11th Air Regiment. The crest of the city of Ostrava is painted on the nose.

Left: The Fleet Air Arm Museum at RNAS Yeovilton displays this former Polish Air Force Lim-2 in North Korean markings. It was imported into the UK in the 1980s and registered G-BMZF but never flew as a private aircraft. *Paul Fiddian*
Right: G-MIGG is a Polish built PZL Lim-5 that was imported into the UK in the 1990s by the Duxford-based Old Flying Machine Company with a view to returning it to the skies. The licence-built MiG-17 is now registered to David Miles and is based at North Weald but has yet to fly in civilian hands.